A TREASURY OF
Charted Designs
FOR NEEDLEWORKERS

141 Motifs Including
Birds, Flowers, Animals, Toys, etc.

Georgia L. Gorham
and Jeanne M. Warth

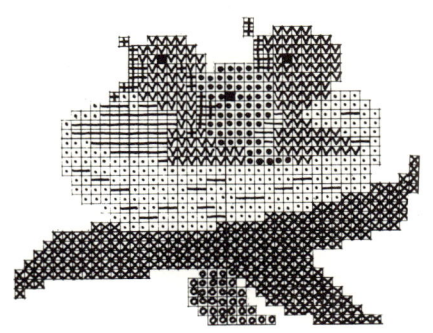

DOVER PUBLICATIONS, INC.
NEW YORK

Published in Canada by General Publishing
Company, Ltd., 30 Lesmill Road, Don Mills,
Toronto, Ontario.
Published in the United Kingdom by Con-
stable and Company, Ltd., 10 Orange Street,
London WC2H 7EG.

*A Treasury of Charted Designs for Needle-
workers* is a new work, first published by
Dover Publications, Inc., in 1977.

International Standard Book Number: 0-486-23558-0
Library of Congress Catalog Card Number: 77-77050

Manufactured in the United States of America
Dover Publications, Inc.
180 Varick Street
New York, N.Y. 10014

INTRODUCTION

This collection consists of 141 motifs charted for ready use in different forms of needlework such as needlepoint, latch-hooking, counted cross-stitch, crochet and knitting. The motifs include those designs most wanted by needleworkers: birds, flowers, animals, toys, fruits and vegetables, buildings, old-fashioned scenes and many more. The book is arranged with similar motifs grouped together; i.e., all of the birds appear on pages 1–6, toys on pages 18–20 and the flowers on pages 21-26.

All of the designs are plotted on easy-to-read grids of ten squares to the inch. Bear in mind that the finished piece of needlework will not be the same size as the charted design unless you happen to be working on fabric that has the same number of threads per inch as the chart has squares per inch. To determine how large a finished design will be, divide the number of stitches in the design by the thread-count of the fabric. For example, if a design that is 112 stitches wide by 140 stitches deep is worked on a 14-count cloth, divide 112 stitches by 14 to get 8 and 140 by 14 to get 10; so the worked design will measure 8" x 10". The same design worked on 22-count fabric would measure approximately 5" x 6½".

Use a single small motif on needlepoint canvas to make a coaster, pincushion, pocket or small picture. Repeat the same design or put several different ones together to make a pillow, a belt or a wall hanging. Latch hook or quick point one design onto heavyweight rug canvas and you will have a pillow. Combine several to make a rug.

The designs can be worked directly onto needlepoint canvas by counting off the correct number of warp and woof squares shown on the chart, each square representing one stitch to be taken on the canvas. If you prefer to put some guidelines on the canvas, make certain that your marking medium is waterproof. Use either non-soluble inks, acrylic paints thinned appropriately with water so as not to clog the holes in the canvas, or oil paints mixed with benzine or turpentine. Felt-tipped pens are very handy, but check the labels carefully because not all felt markers are waterproof. It is a good idea to experiment with any writing materials on a piece of scrap canvas to make certain that all material is waterproof. There is nothing worse than having a bit of ink run onto the needle-point as you are blocking it.

For counted cross-stitch, select an evenweave fabric such as cotton aida or hardanger cloth. Each square on the chart represents one cross-stitch taken over the intersection of the threads of the fabric. When working with an evenweave linen in which there are some thin threads and some nubbier or fatter ones, the cross-stitch is worked over two threads each way. Make certain that all of the stitches cross in the same direction. Gingham or other checkered material can also be used for cross-stitch by making the crosses over the checks from corner to corner. If you wish to embroider a cross-stitch design onto a fabric which does not have an evenweave, baste a lightweight Penelope canvas to the fabric. The design can then be worked from the chart by making crosses over the double mesh of the canvas, being careful not to catch the threads of the canvas in the sewing. When the design is completed, the basting stitches are removed, and the horizontal and then the vertical threads of the canvas are removed, one strand at a time, with a tweezers. The cross-stitch design will remain on the fabric.

Charted designs can be worked in duplicate

stitch over the squares formed by stockinette stitch in knitting or afghan stitch in crochet. The patterns can also be knitted directly into the work by working with more than one color, as in Fair Isle knitting. The wool not in use is always stranded across the back of the work. When it has to be stranded over more than five stitches, it should be twisted around the wool in use on every third stitch, thus preventing long strands at the back of the work. When a number of colors are used, a method known as "motif knitting" is employed. In this method short lengths of wool are cut and wound on bobbins, using a separate bobbin for each color and twist-ing the colors where they meet to avoid gaps in the work, as in knitting argyle socks.

Each of the designs has its own color key. The colors, however, are merely suggestions. You should feel free to substitute your own colors for the ones indicated, thereby creating a design which is uniquely yours. If you decide to create a new color scheme, work it out in detail before beginning a project. To give you a good idea of how the finished project will look, put tracing paper over the design in the book and experiment with your own colors on the tracing paper.

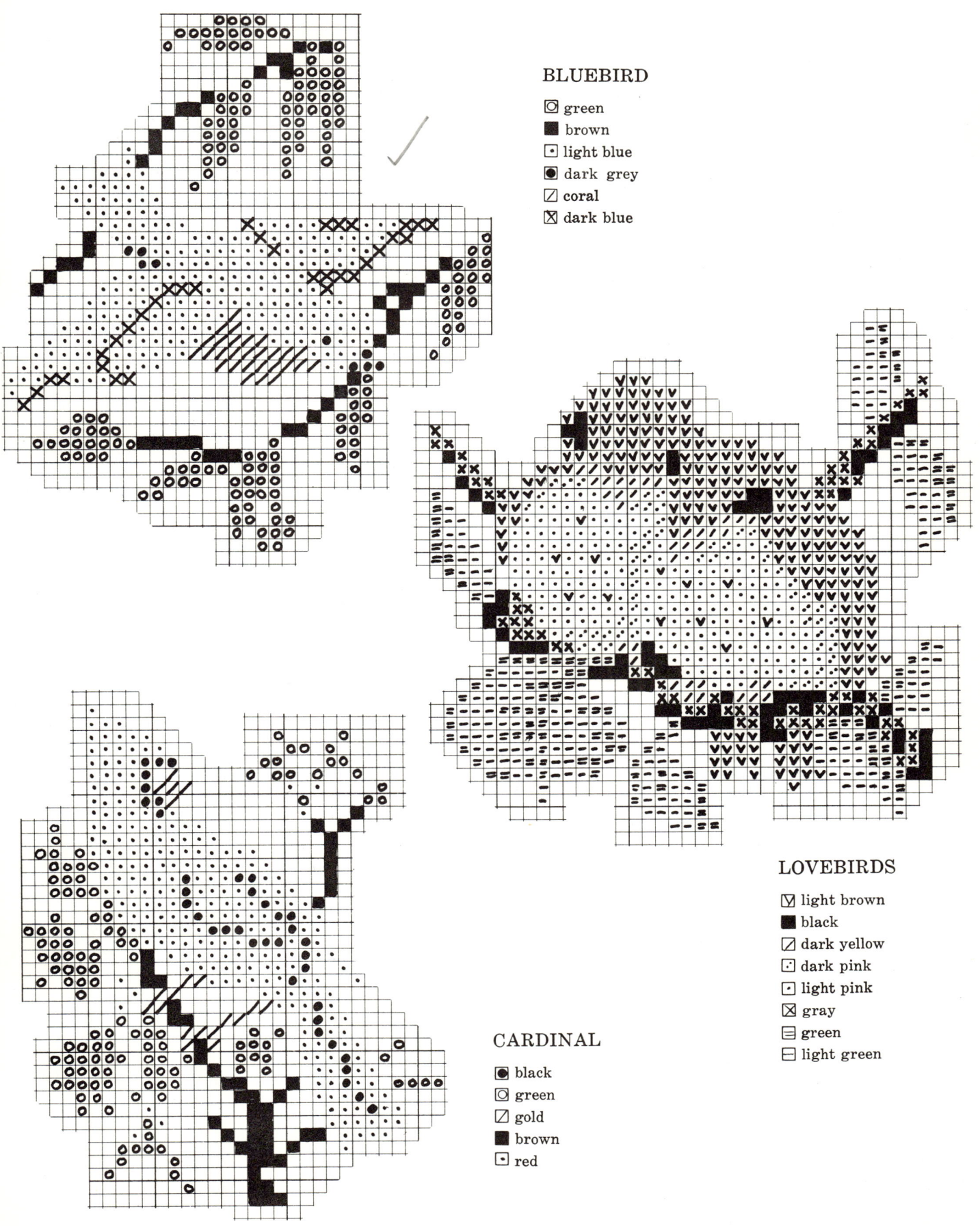

BLUEBIRD

- ⊙ green
- ■ brown
- ⊡ light blue
- ◉ dark grey
- ⧄ coral
- ⊠ dark blue

LOVEBIRDS

- ⊻ light brown
- ■ black
- ⧄ dark yellow
- ⊡ dark pink
- ⊡ light pink
- ⊠ gray
- ⊟ green
- ⊟ light green

CARDINAL

- ◉ black
- ⊙ green
- ⧄ gold
- ■ brown
- ⊡ red

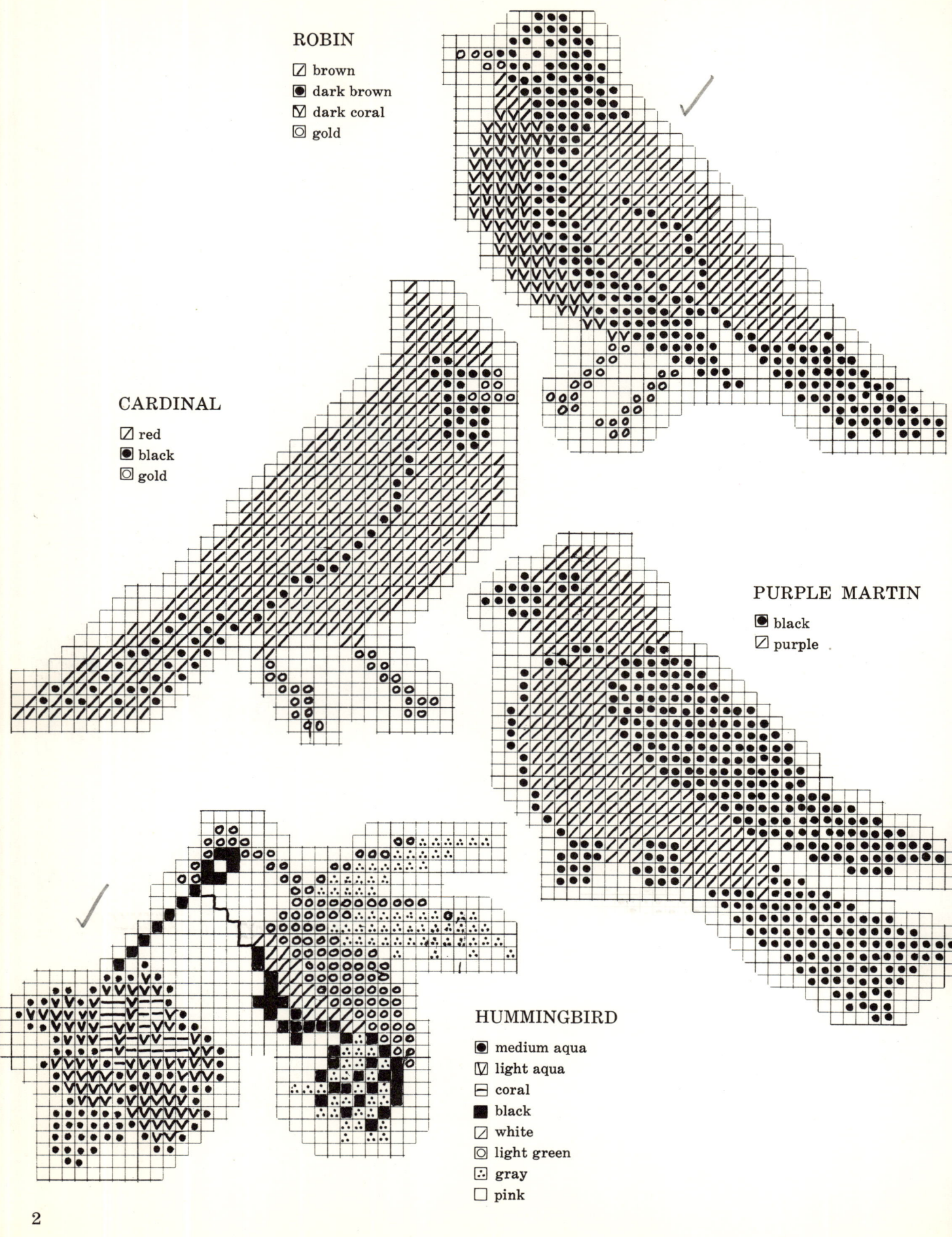

ROBIN

☑ brown
◉ dark brown
Ⓥ dark coral
◎ gold

CARDINAL

☑ red
◉ black
◎ gold

PURPLE MARTIN

◉ black
☑ purple

HUMMINGBIRD

◉ medium aqua
Ⓥ light aqua
⊟ coral
■ black
☑ white
◎ light green
⣿ gray
☐ pink

BIRD

◣ dark green
◎ light green
⊠ medium brown
⊞ yellow
⊟ coral
☐ pink
◉ medium aqua
Ⅴ light aqua
■ black

ROBIN

◉ medium brown
· light brown
■ dark brown
◎ green
⊠ coral
⟋ gold

WOODPECKER

◉ medium brown
· light brown
⊟ red
Ⅴ white
⊠ black

BIRDS

◉ medium aqua
Ⅴ light aqua
◎ light green
⟋ white

3

OWL

- ⊟ light brown
- ■ black
- ◉ dark brown
- ⊘ medium brown
- ⊡ white
- Ⓥ green

OWL

- ⊡ tan
- ⊘ coral
- ◉ brown

30 st wide ÷ 18 = 2"
43 st long ÷ 18 = 3"

OWL

- ⊘ beige
- ◉ brown

OWL

- ◉ brown
- ⊘ coral

4

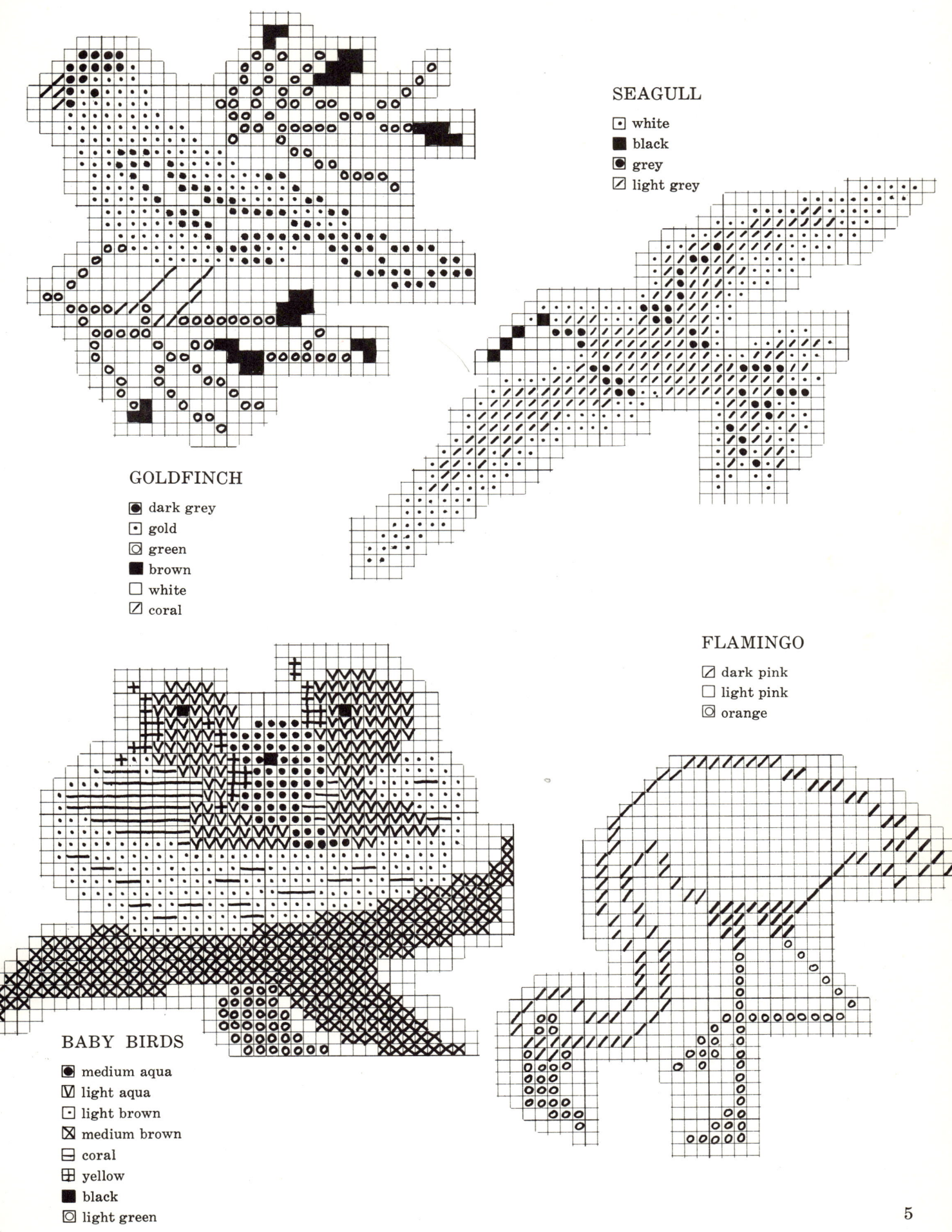

SEAGULL

- ⊡ white
- ■ black
- ◉ grey
- ⊘ light grey

GOLDFINCH

- ◉ dark grey
- ⊡ gold
- ⊙ green
- ■ brown
- ☐ white
- ⊘ coral

FLAMINGO

- ⊘ dark pink
- ☐ light pink
- ⊙ orange

BABY BIRDS

- ◉ medium aqua
- Ⅴ light aqua
- ⊡ light brown
- ⊠ medium brown
- ⊟ coral
- ⊞ yellow
- ■ black
- ⊙ light green

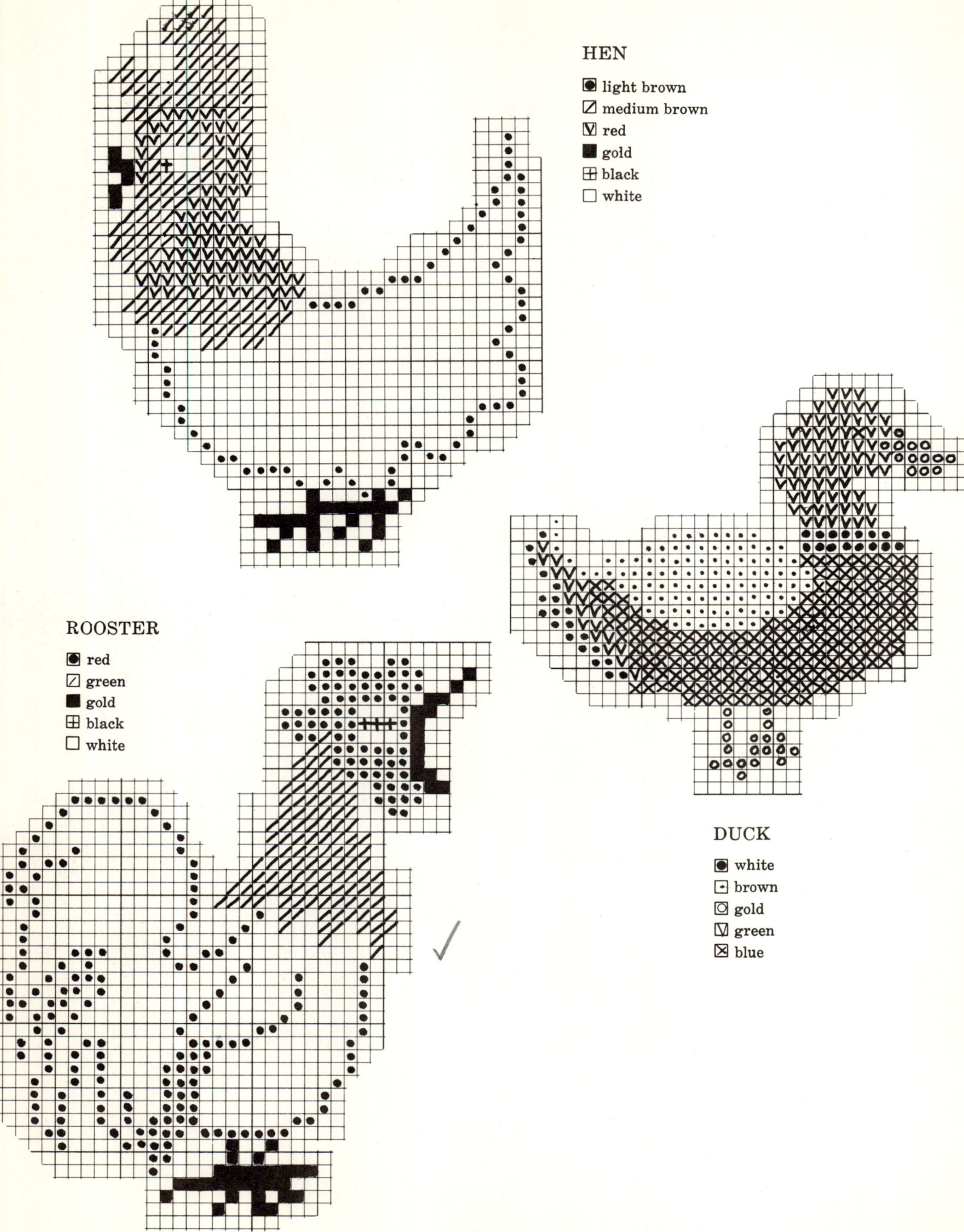

HEN

- ◉ light brown
- ▨ medium brown
- ⋁ red
- ■ gold
- ⊞ black
- ☐ white

ROOSTER

- ◉ red
- ▨ green
- ■ gold
- ⊞ black
- ☐ white

DUCK

- ◉ white
- ⊡ brown
- ◎ gold
- ⋁ green
- ⊠ blue

6

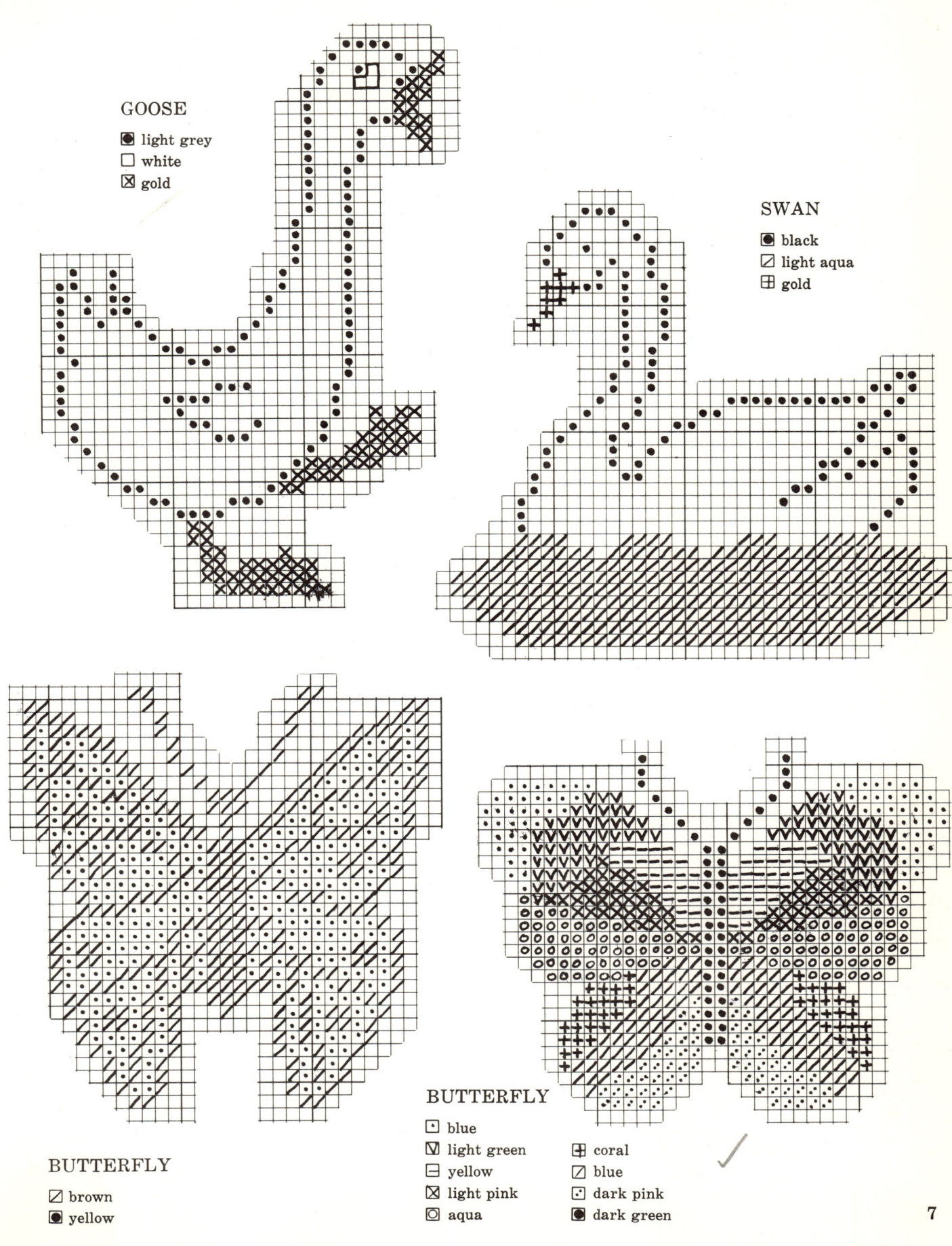

GOOSE

- ◉ light grey
- ☐ white
- ☒ gold

SWAN

- ◉ black
- ◨ light aqua
- ⊞ gold

BUTTERFLY

- ◨ brown
- ◉ yellow

BUTTERFLY

- ⊡ blue
- Ⓥ light green
- ⊟ yellow
- ☒ light pink
- Ⓞ aqua
- ⊞ coral
- ◨ blue
- ⊡ dark pink
- ◉ dark green

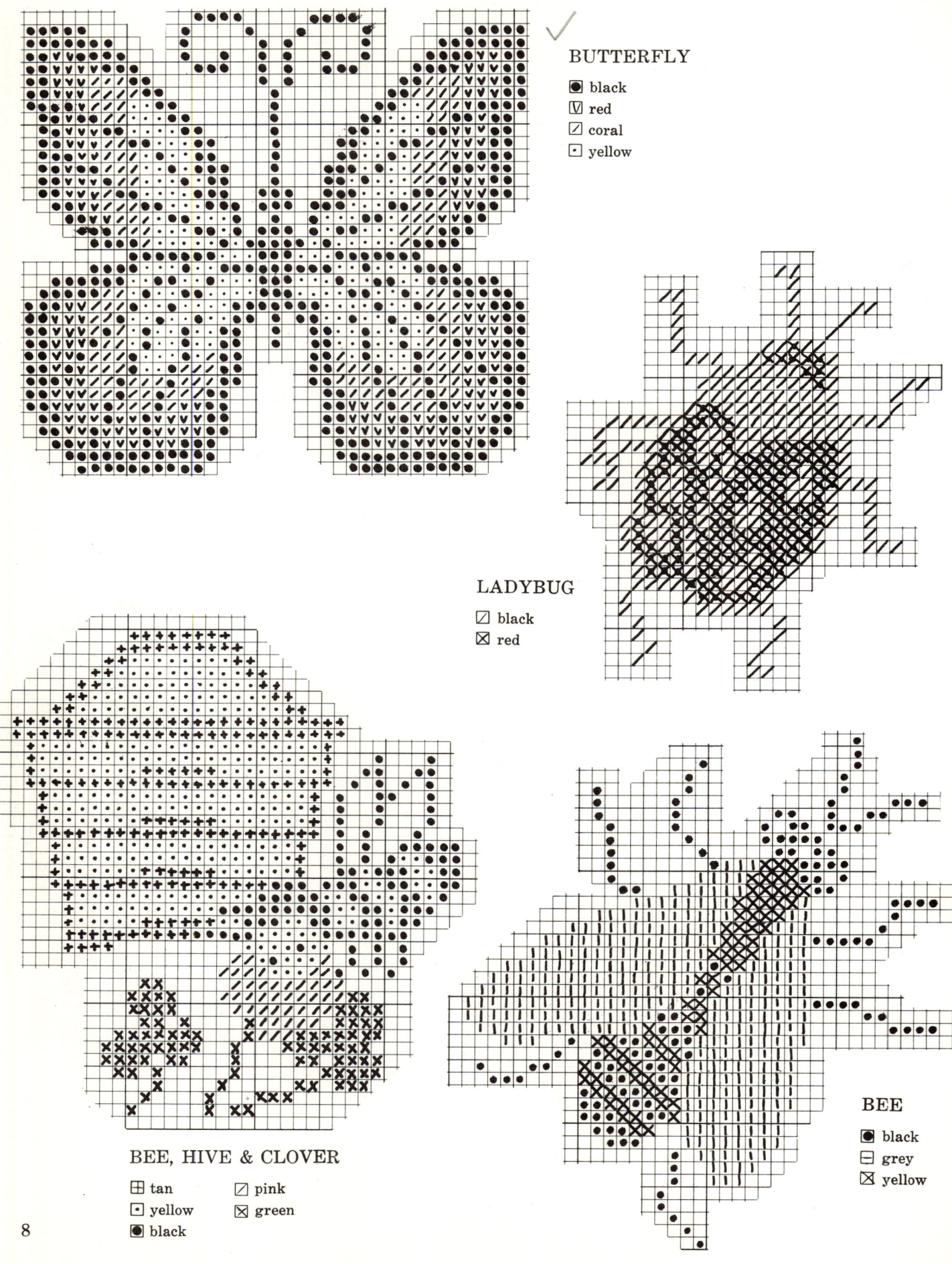

BUTTERFLY

- ⬤ black
- Ⅴ red
- ☑ coral
- • yellow

LADYBUG

- ☑ black
- ⊠ red

BEE

- ⬤ black
- ⊟ grey
- ⊠ yellow

BEE, HIVE & CLOVER

- ⊞ tan
- ☑ pink
- • yellow
- ⊠ green
- ⬤ black

8

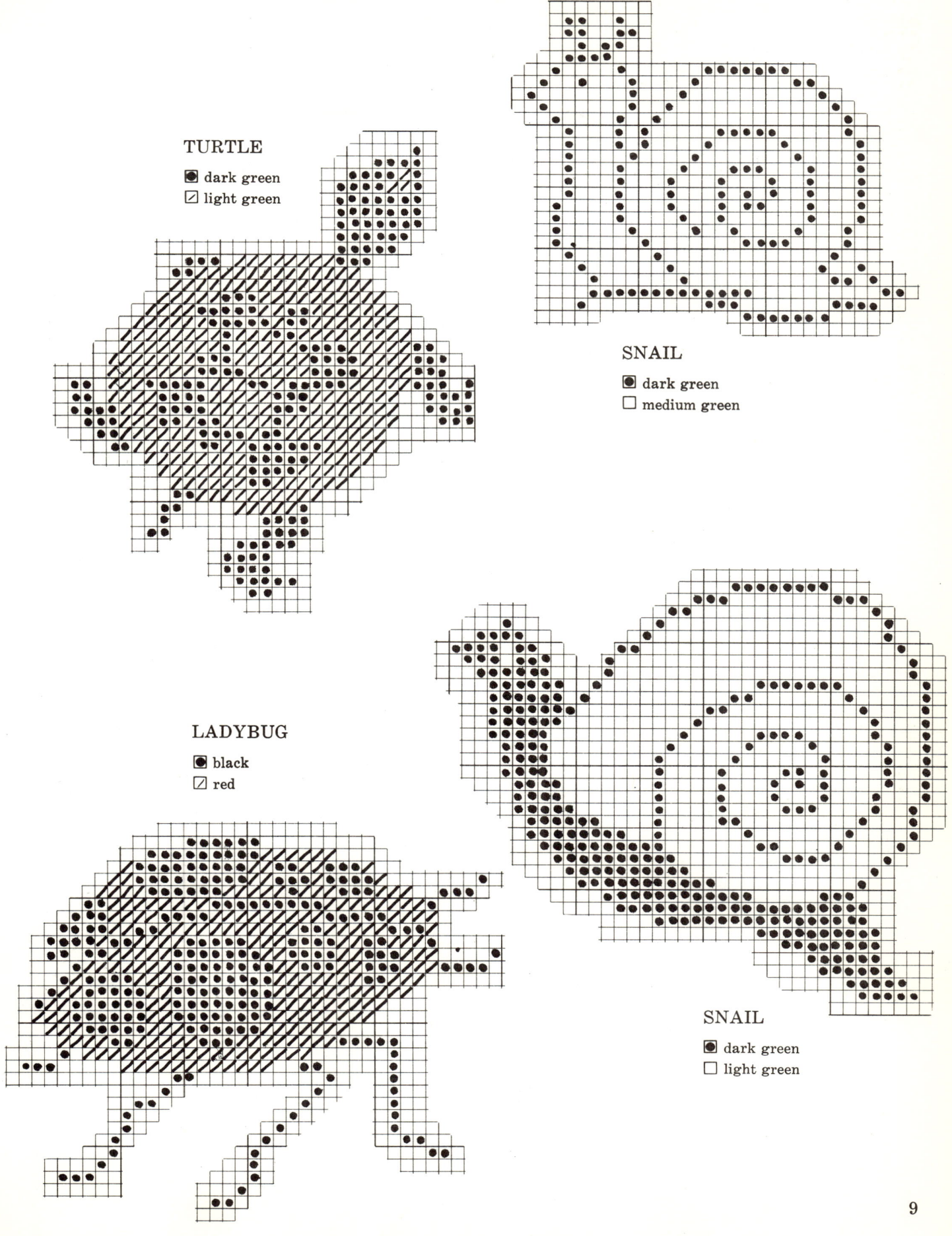

TURTLE
● dark green
⊘ light green

SNAIL
● dark green
☐ medium green

LADYBUG
● black
⊘ red

SNAIL
● dark green
☐ light green

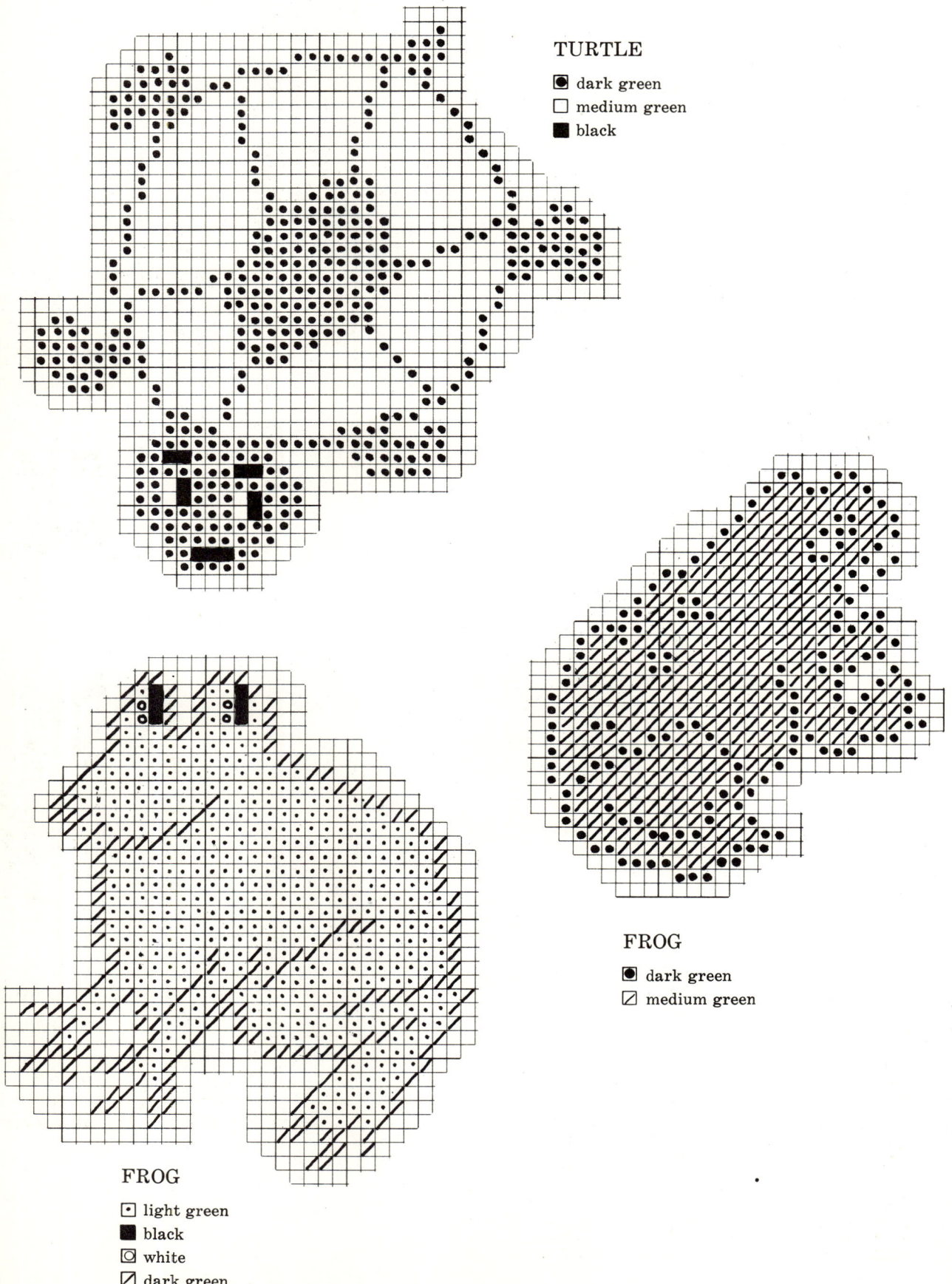

TURTLE

- ◉ dark green
- ☐ medium green
- ■ black

FROG

- ◉ dark green
- ▨ medium green

FROG

- ⊡ light green
- ■ black
- ⊙ white
- ▨ dark green

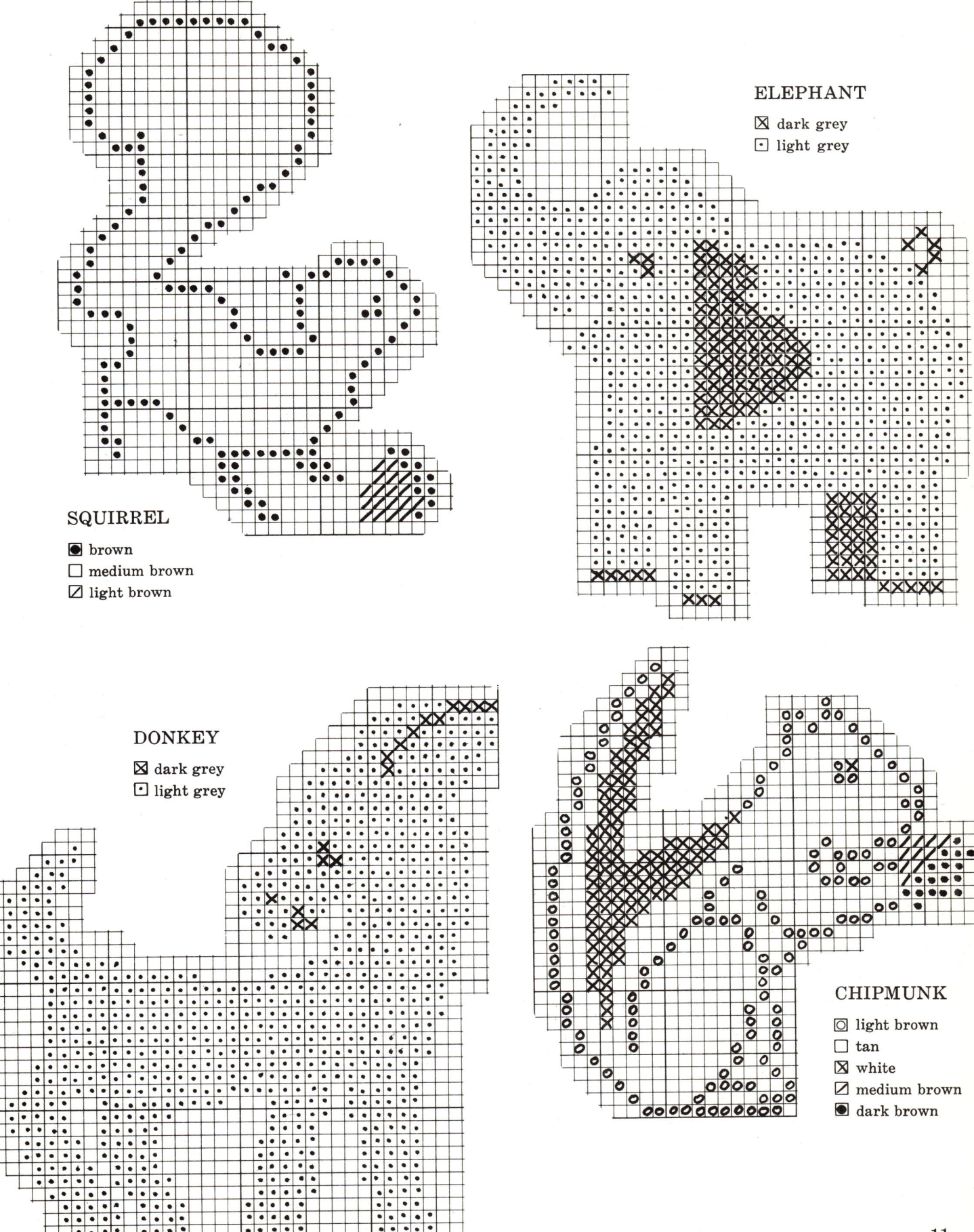

ELEPHANT

⊠ dark grey
· light grey

SQUIRREL

● brown
☐ medium brown
⧄ light brown

DONKEY

⊠ dark grey
· light grey

CHIPMUNK

◎ light brown
☐ tan
⊠ white
⧄ medium brown
● dark brown

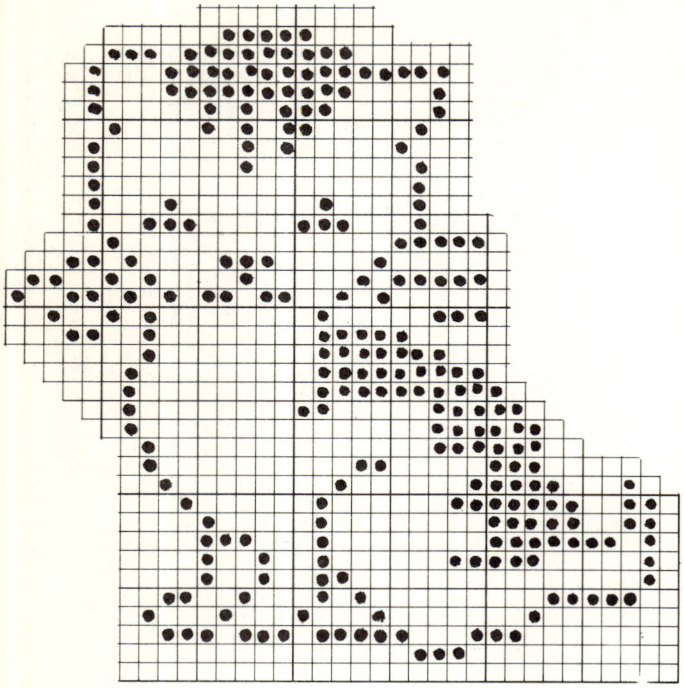

CAT

◉ brown
☐ tan

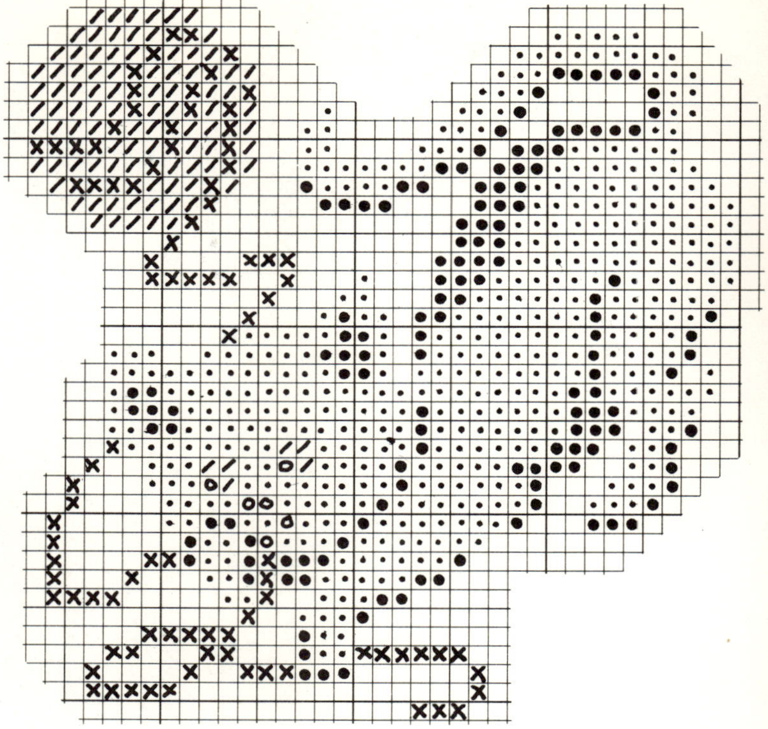

CAT WITH YARN

⊡ tan
◉ brown
▨ light green
☒ dark green
⊙ black

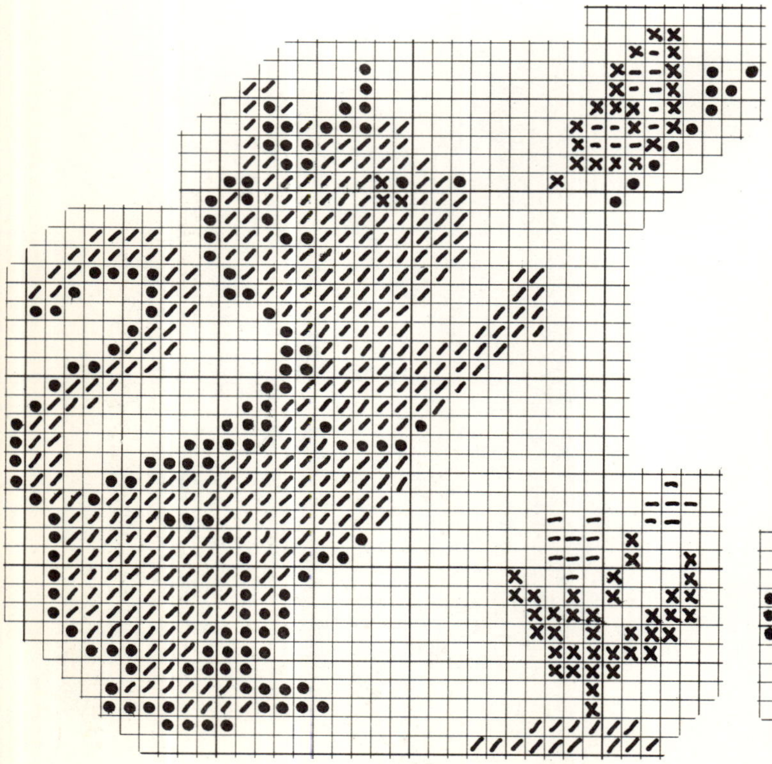

CAT WITH BUTTERFLY

◉ black   ☒ green
▨ grey   ⊟ pink

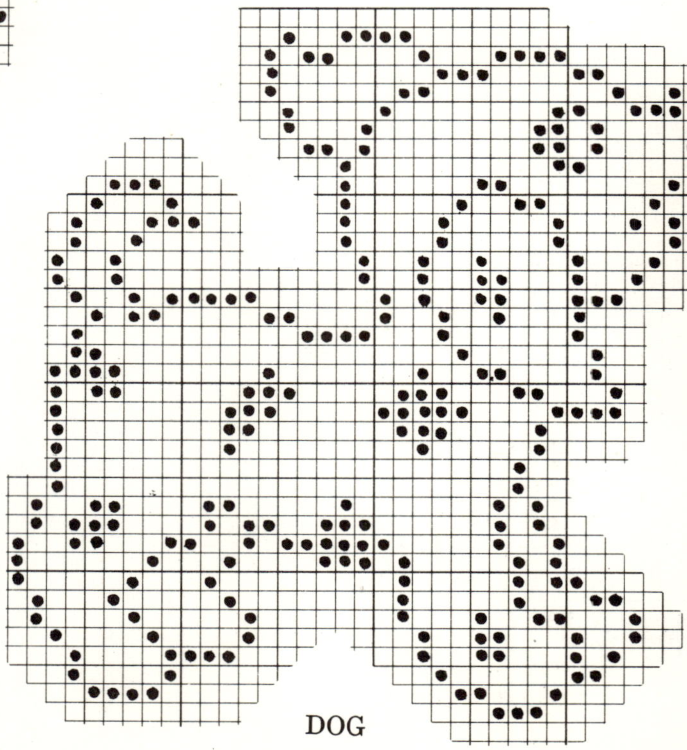

DOG

◉ brown
☐ tan

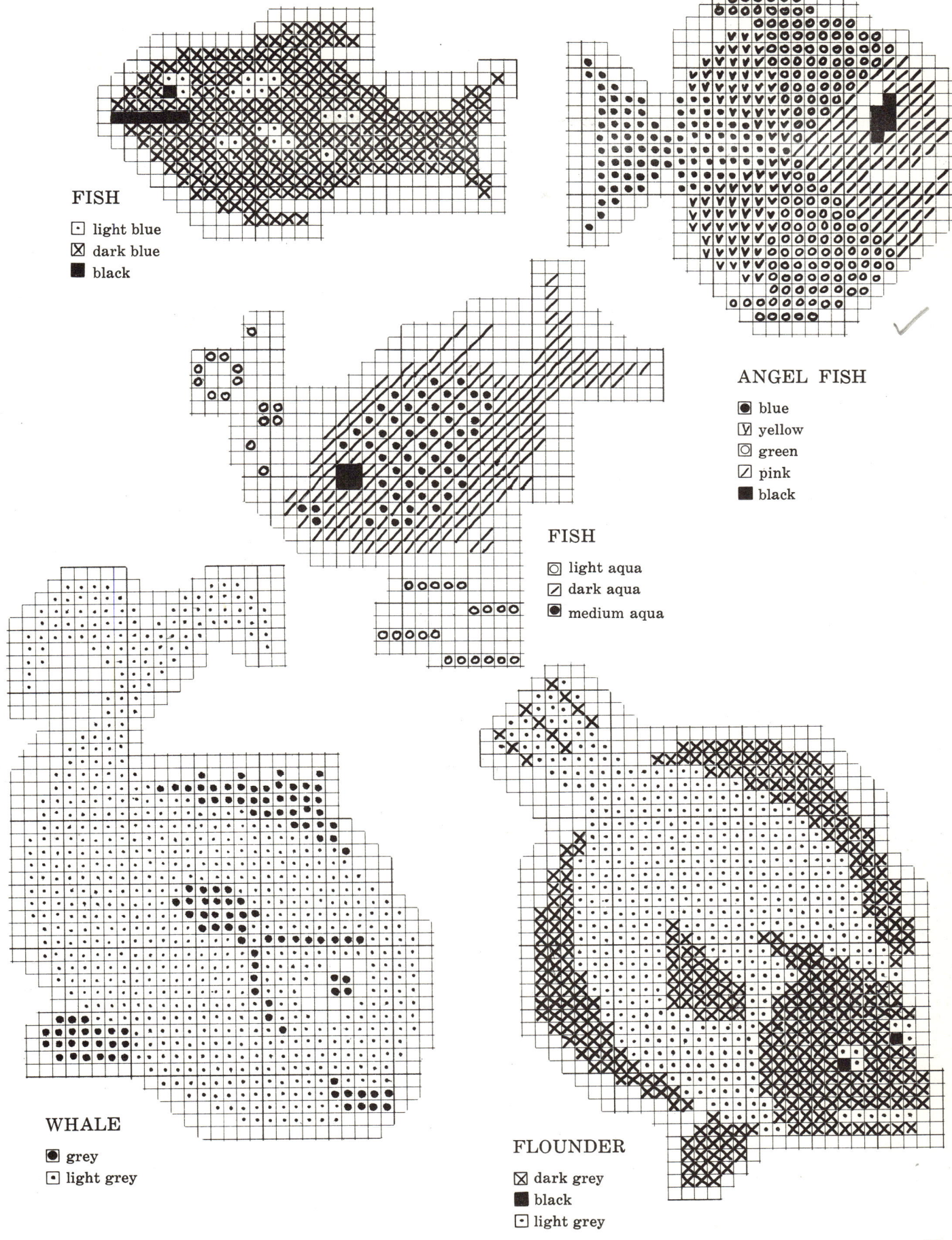

FISH

⊡ light blue
☒ dark blue
■ black

ANGEL FISH

◉ blue
Ⓨ yellow
Ⓞ green
⊘ pink
■ black

FISH

Ⓞ light aqua
⊘ dark aqua
◉ medium aqua

WHALE

◉ grey
⊡ light grey

FLOUNDER

☒ dark grey
■ black
⊡ light grey

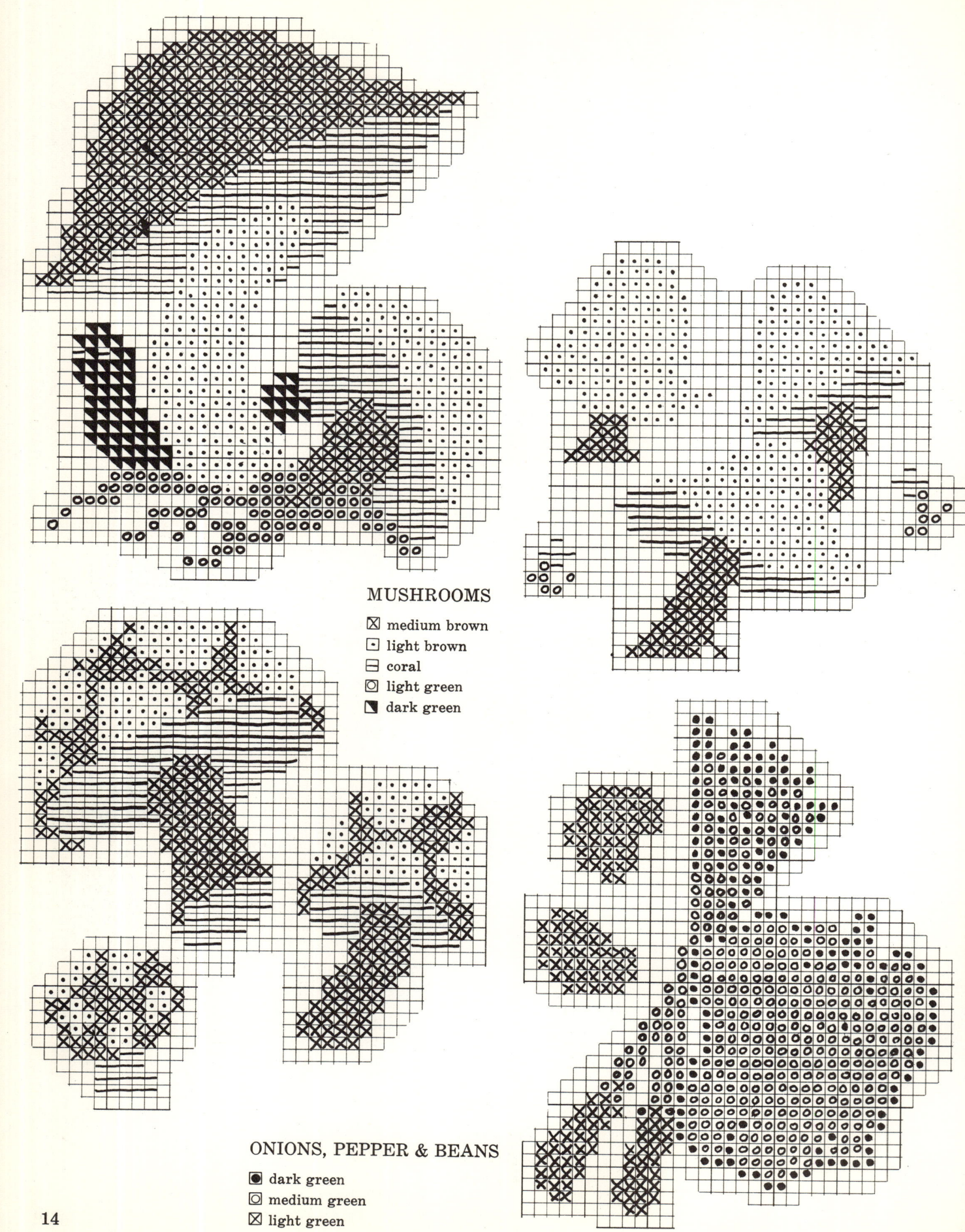

MUSHROOMS

⊠ medium brown
⊡ light brown
⊟ coral
◉ light green
◣ dark green

ONIONS, PEPPER & BEANS

◉ dark green
⊙ medium green
⊠ light green

14

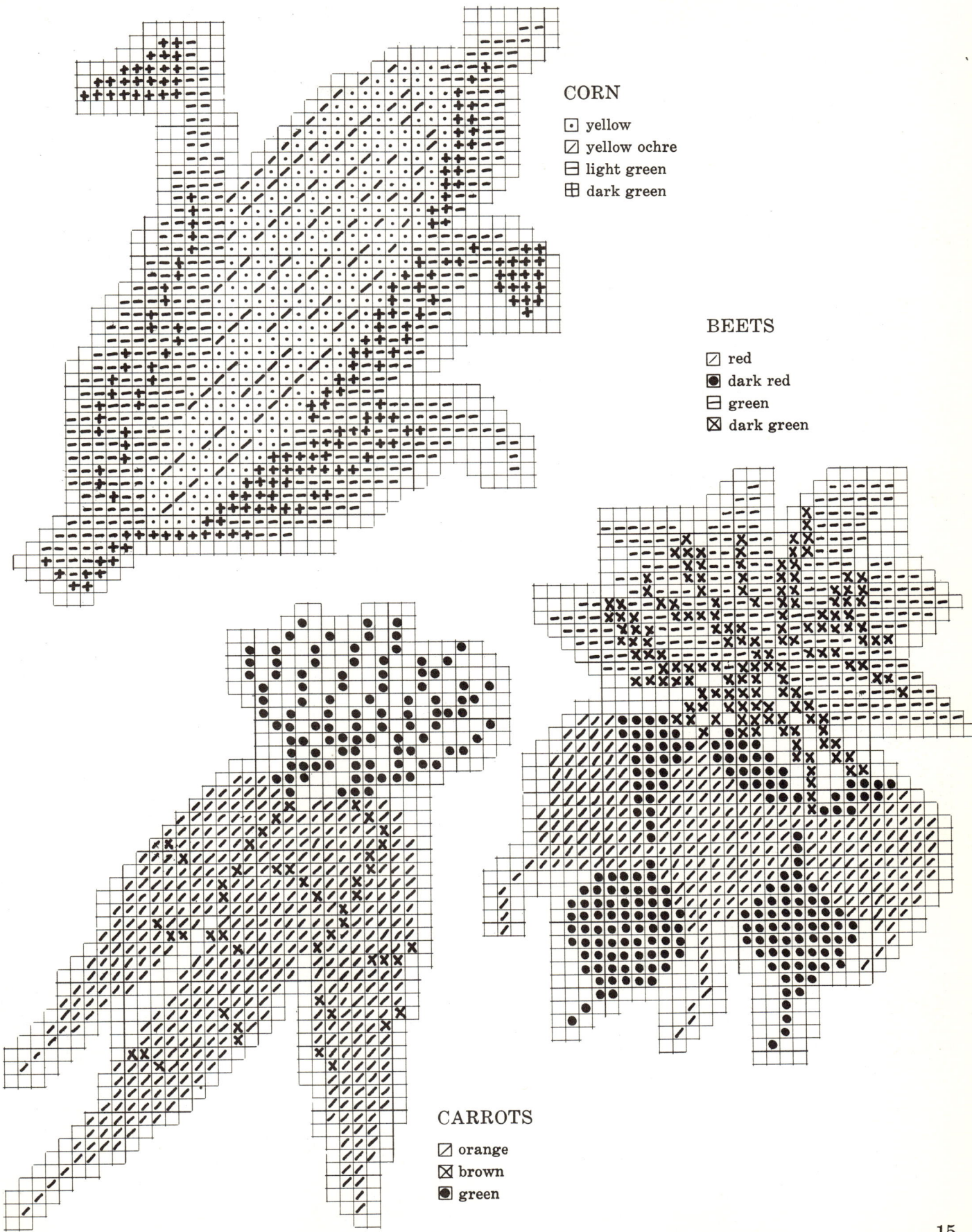

CORN

⊡ yellow
☑ yellow ochre
⊟ light green
⊞ dark green

BEETS

☑ red
⬤ dark red
⊟ green
☒ dark green

CARROTS

☑ orange
☒ brown
⬤ green

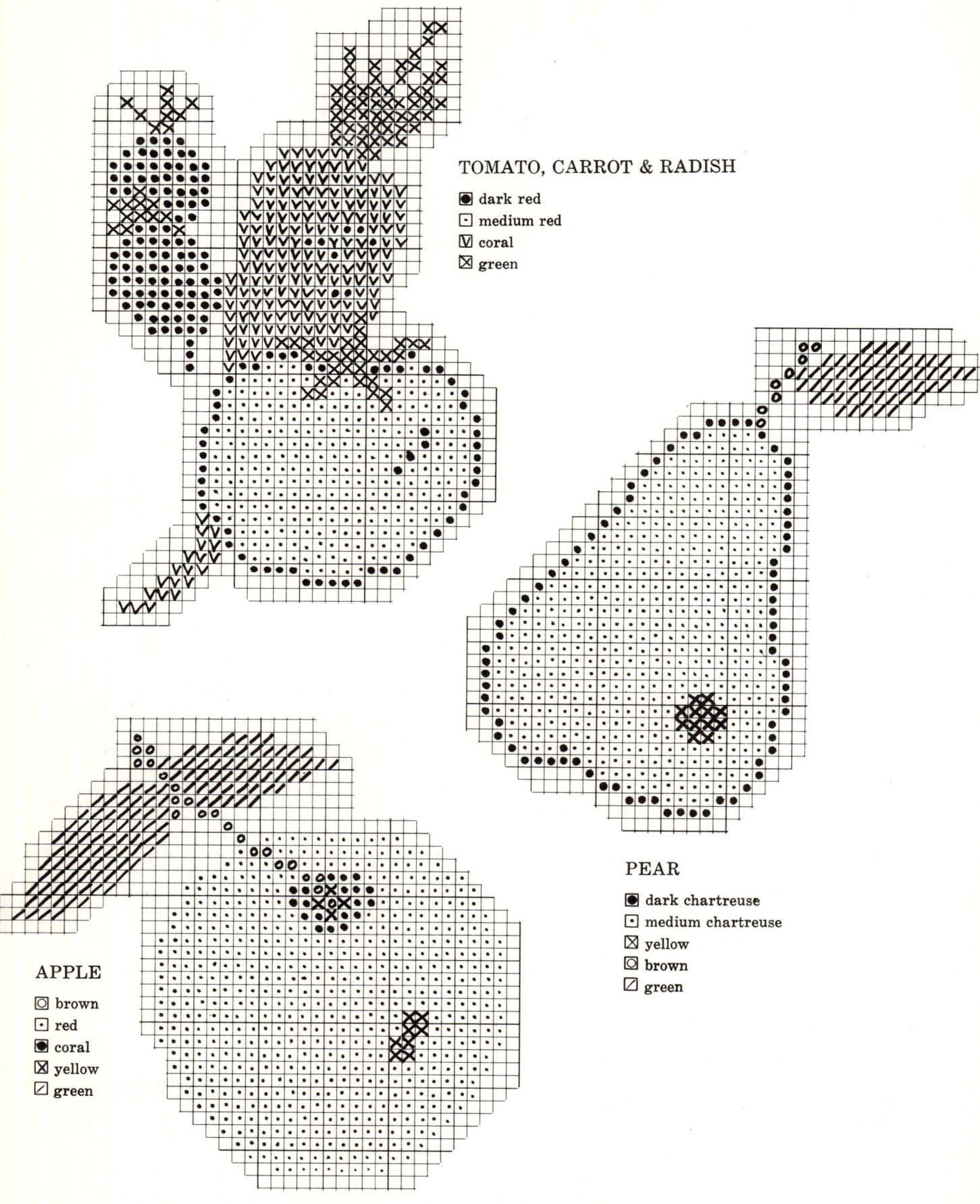

TOMATO, CARROT & RADISH

- ◉ dark red
- ⊡ medium red
- ⋁ coral
- ⊠ green

PEAR

- ◉ dark chartreuse
- ⊡ medium chartreuse
- ⊠ yellow
- ◎ brown
- ⧄ green

APPLE

- ◎ brown
- ⊡ red
- ◉ coral
- ⊠ yellow
- ⧄ green

16

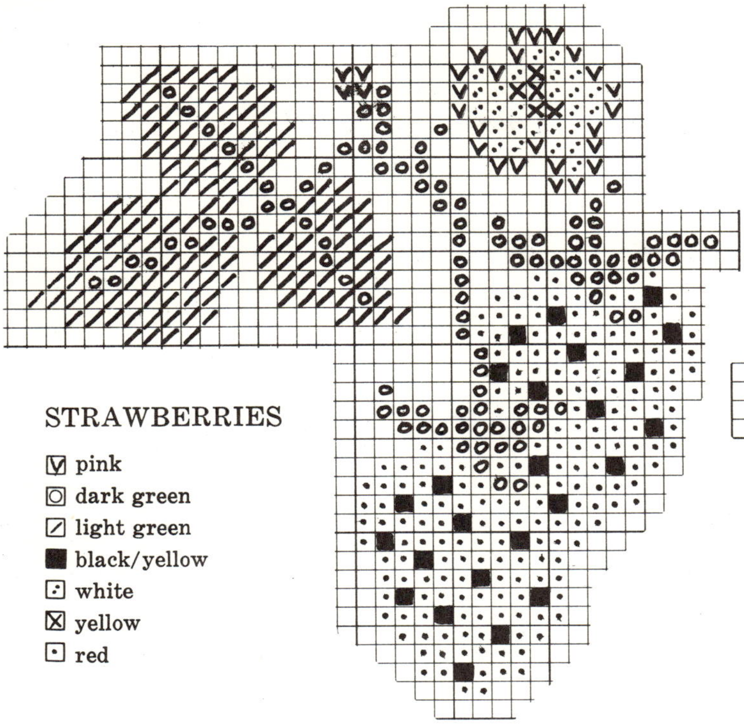

STRAWBERRIES

- ⍌ pink
- ◎ dark green
- ⟋ light green
- ■ black/yellow
- ⊡ white
- ⊠ yellow
- ⊡ red

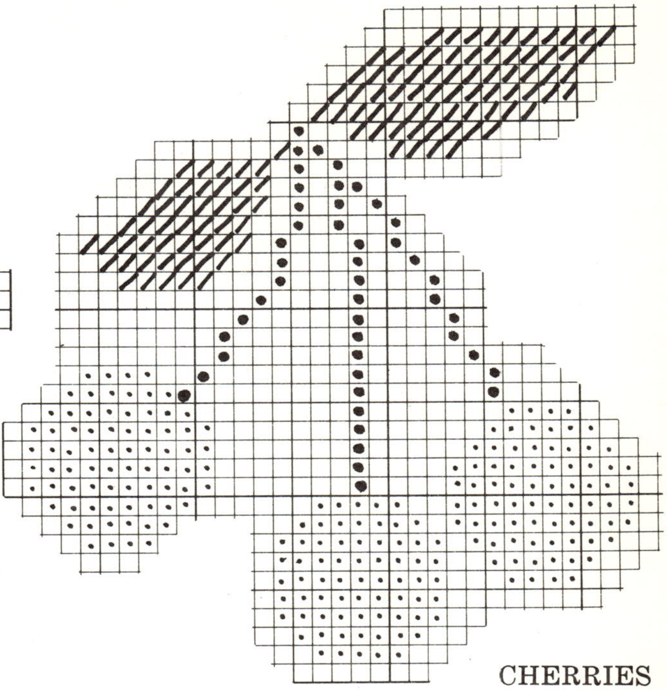

CHERRIES

- ⊡ red
- ● dark green
- ⟋ light green

WATERMELON

- ⊡ white
- ● black
- ⟋ light green
- ⊠ dark green
- ⊟ red

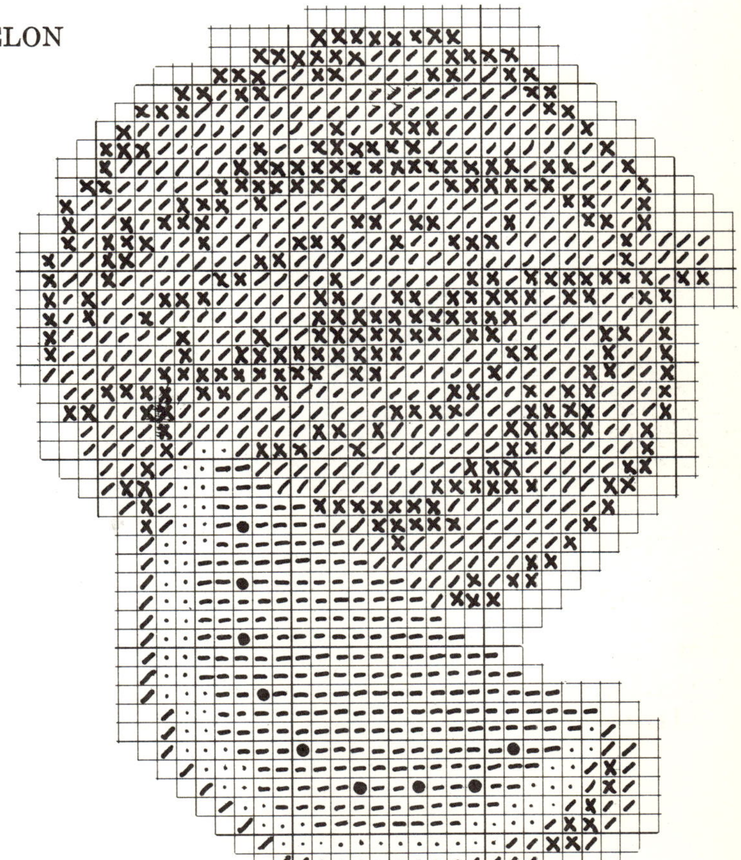

LEMONS

- ● dark yellow
- ⊡ light yellow
- ◎ dark green
- ⟋ light green

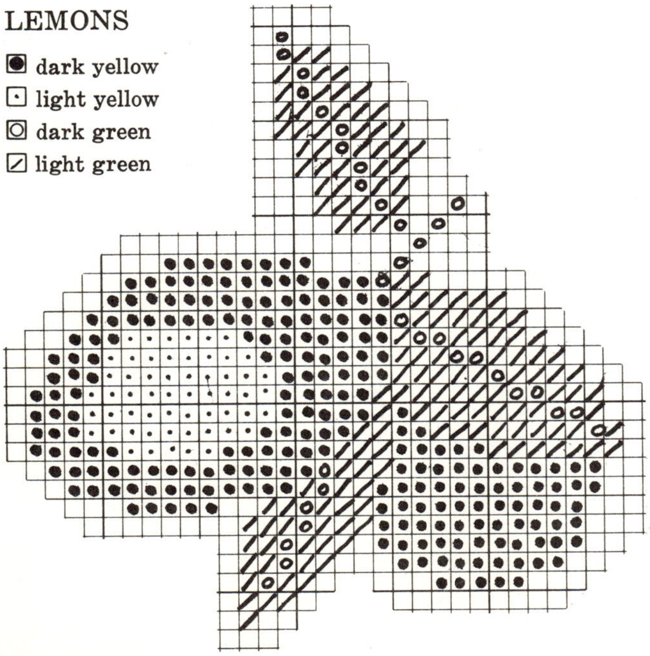

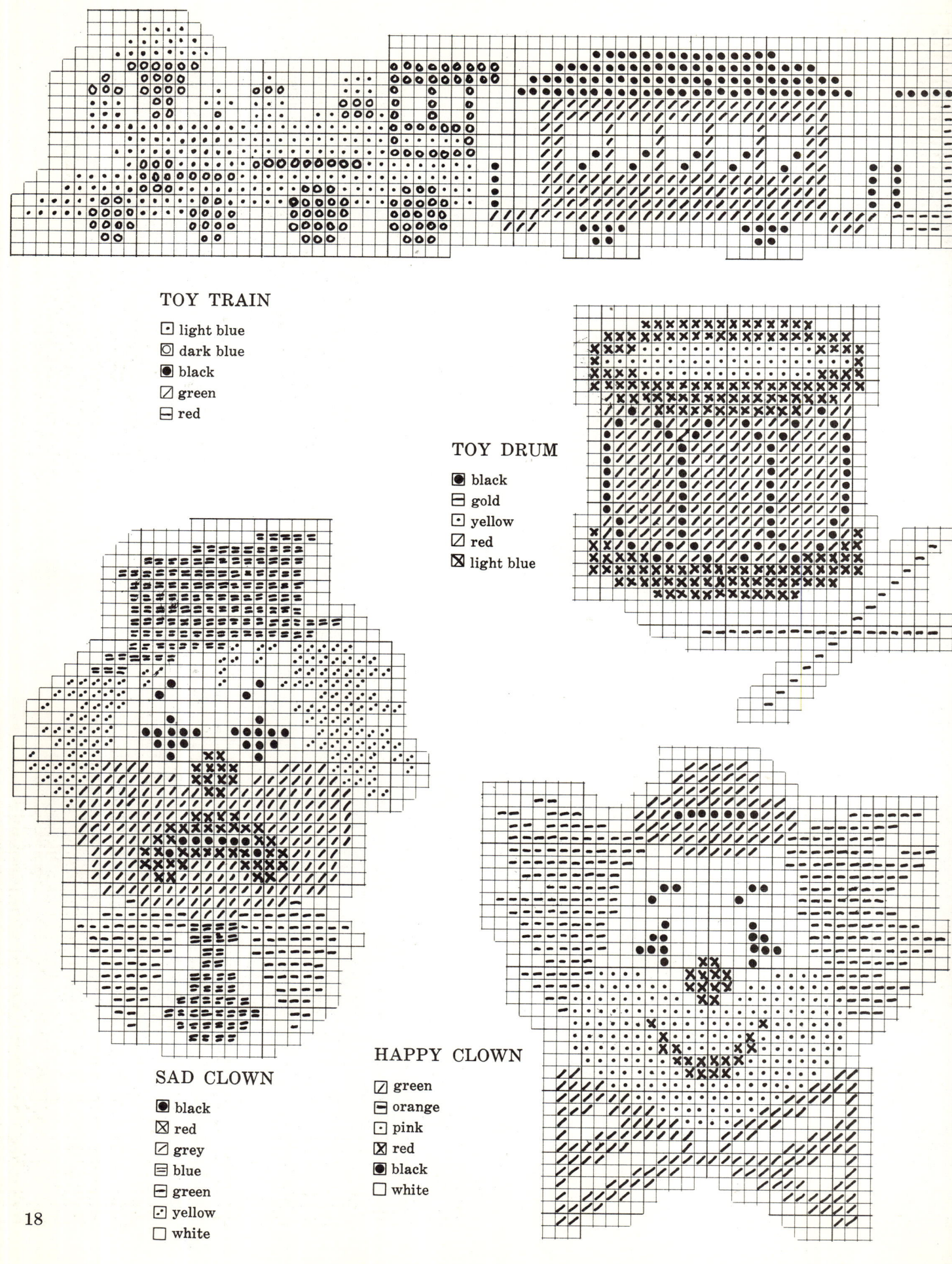

TOY TRAIN

⊡ light blue
◉ dark blue
● black
⊘ green
⊟ red

TOY DRUM

● black
⊟ gold
⊡ yellow
⊘ red
☒ light blue

SAD CLOWN

● black
☒ red
⊘ grey
⊟ blue
⊖ green
⊡ yellow
☐ white

HAPPY CLOWN

⊘ green
⊟ orange
⊡ pink
☒ red
● black
☐ white

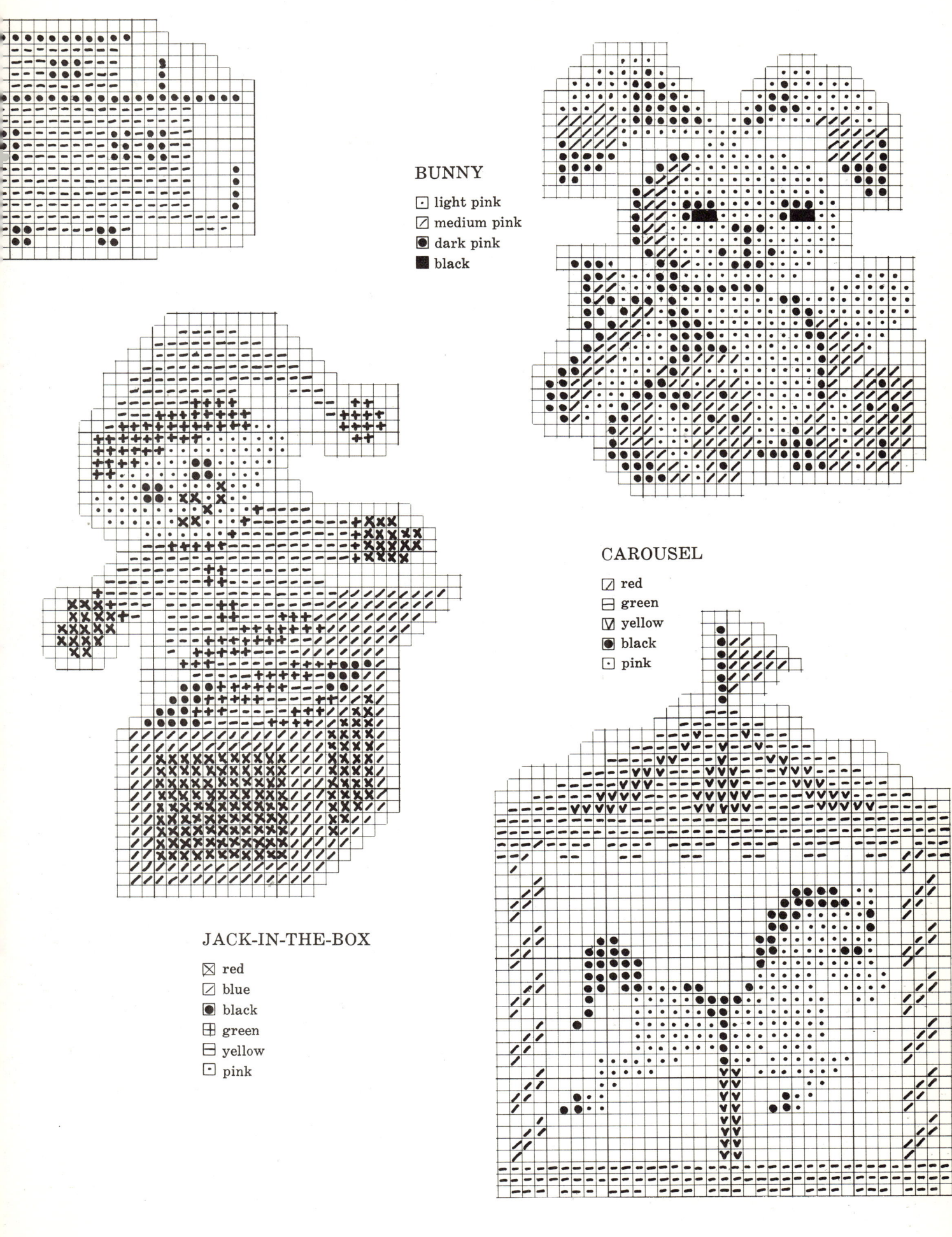

BUNNY

- ⊡ light pink
- ⊘ medium pink
- ⊙ dark pink
- ◼ black

CAROUSEL

- ⊘ red
- ⊟ green
- ⊻ yellow
- ⊙ black
- ⊡ pink

JACK-IN-THE-BOX

- ⊠ red
- ⊘ blue
- ⊙ black
- ⊞ green
- ⊟ yellow
- ⊡ pink

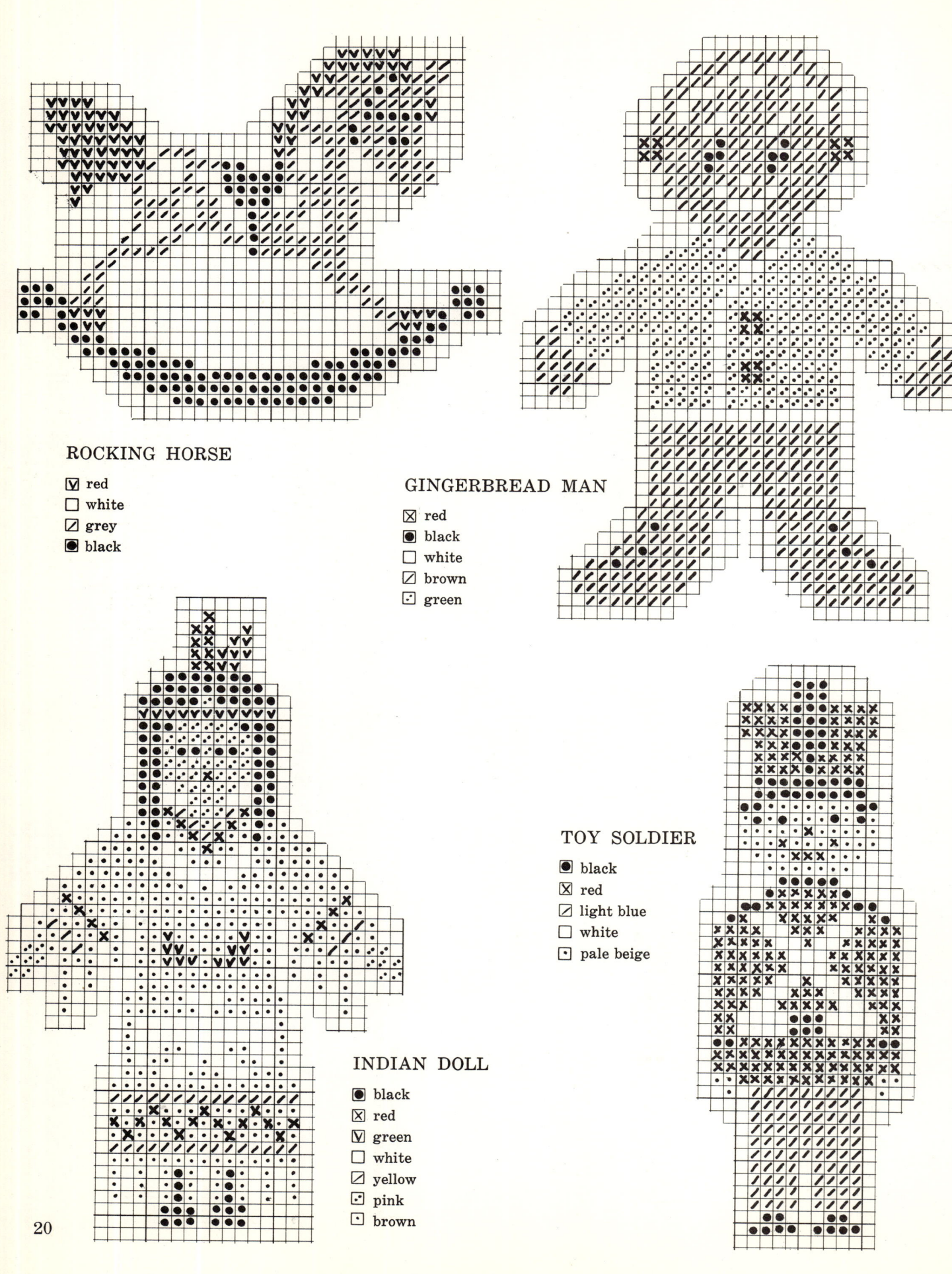

ROCKING HORSE

- ☑ red
- ☐ white
- ☑ grey
- ● black

GINGERBREAD MAN

- ☒ red
- ● black
- ☐ white
- ☑ brown
- ⦁ green

INDIAN DOLL

- ● black
- ☒ red
- ☑ green
- ☐ white
- ☑ yellow
- ⦁ pink
- ⦁ brown

TOY SOLDIER

- ● black
- ☒ red
- ☑ light blue
- ☐ white
- ⦁ pale beige

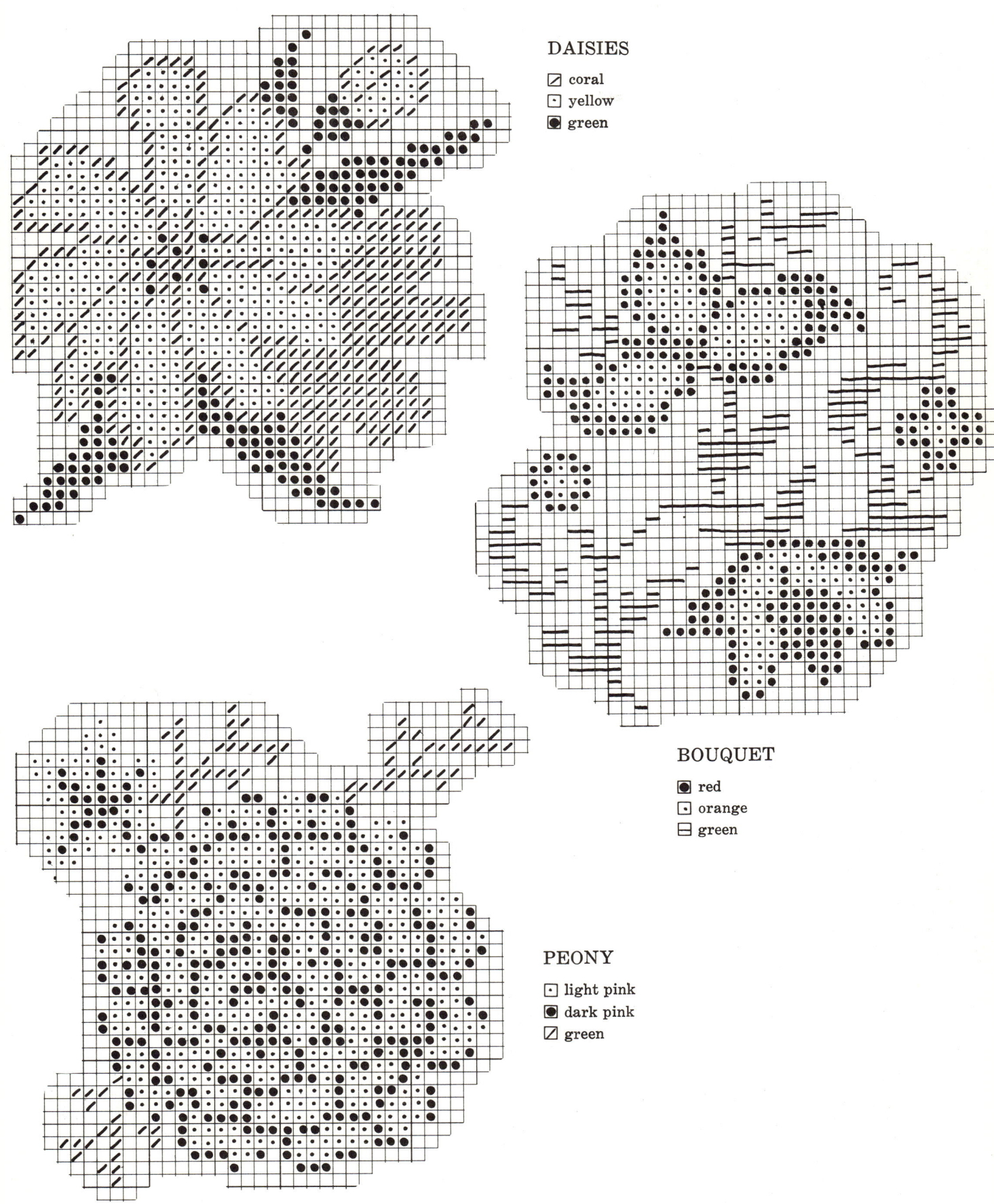

DAISIES

☑ coral
⊡ yellow
⬤ green

BOUQUET

⬤ red
⊡ orange
⊟ green

PEONY

⊡ light pink
⬤ dark pink
☑ green

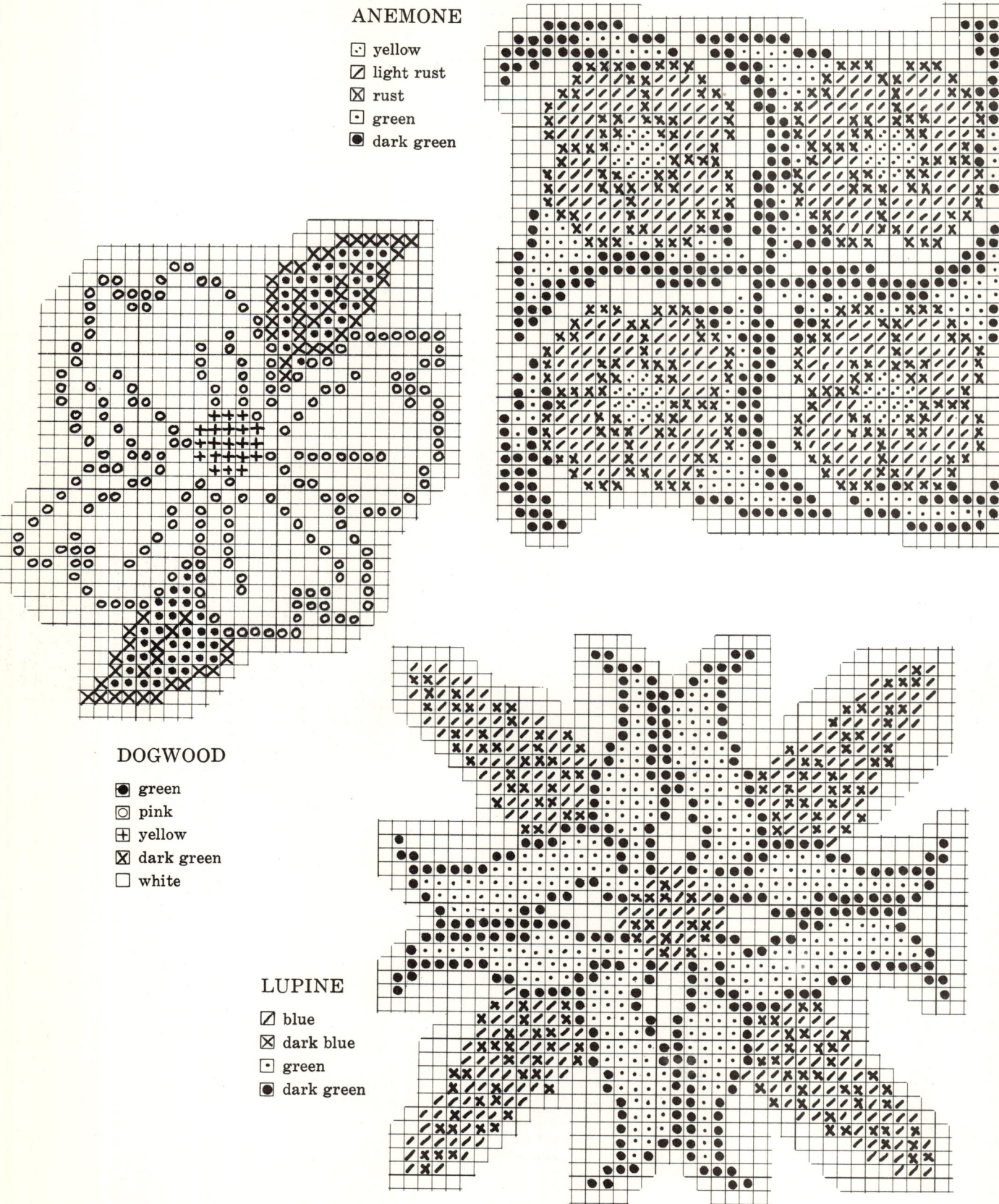

ANEMONE

⊡ yellow
⊘ light rust
☒ rust
· green
● dark green

DOGWOOD

● green
⊘ pink
⊞ yellow
☒ dark green
☐ white

LUPINE

⊘ blue
☒ dark blue
· green
● dark green

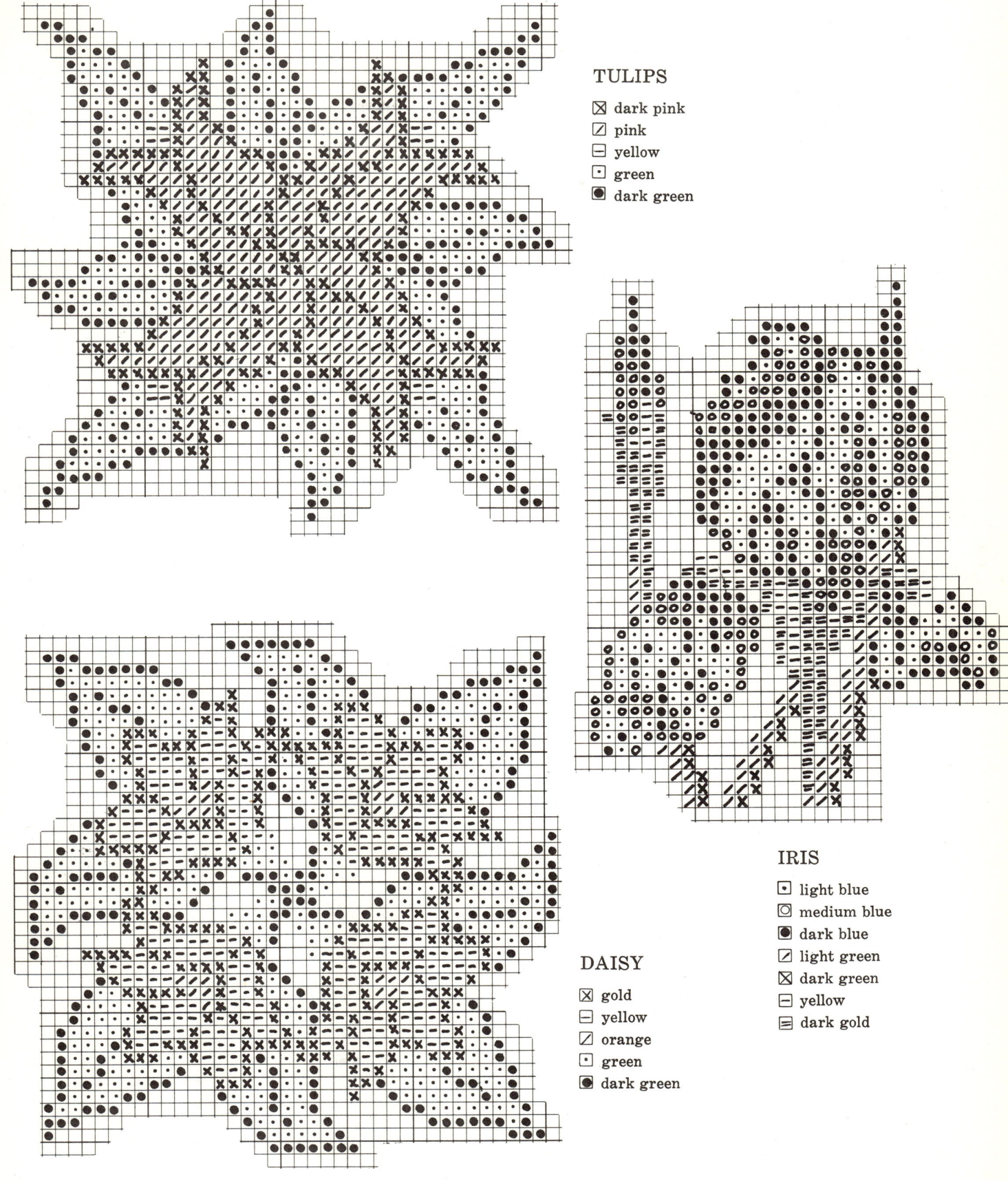

TULIPS

☒ dark pink
☑ pink
⊟ yellow
⊡ green
⬤ dark green

IRIS

⊡ light blue
◎ medium blue
◉ dark blue
☑ light green
☒ dark green
⊟ yellow
⊟ dark gold

DAISY

☒ gold
⊟ yellow
☑ orange
⊡ green
⬤ dark green

□ blue
▤ dark blue
⊡ yellow
⊡ light green
⊻ dark green
⊿ red
⊠ dark red

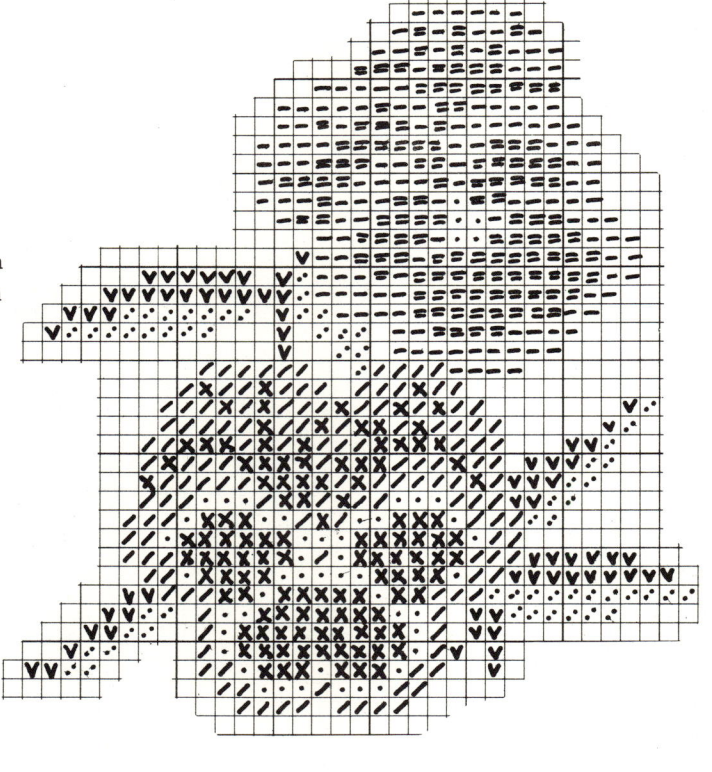

FLOWER

◎ yellow
⊠ pink
⊡ orange
⊿ light green
⬤ green

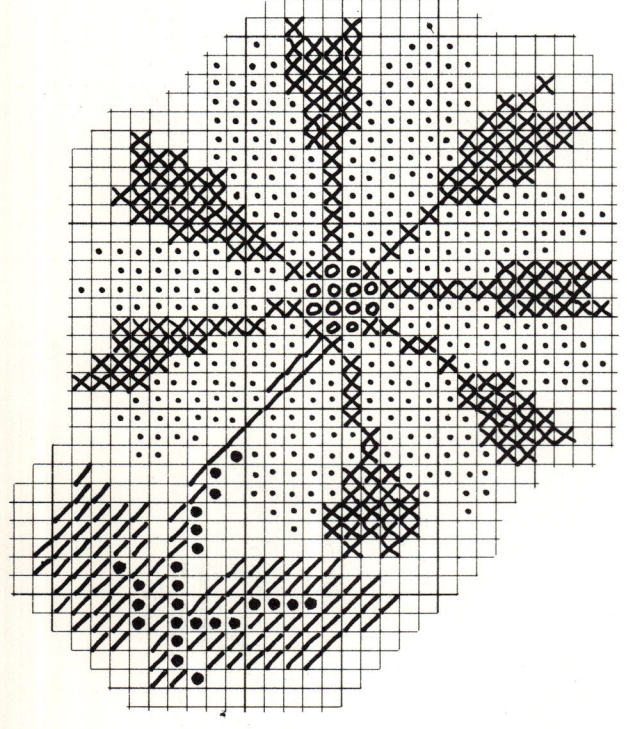

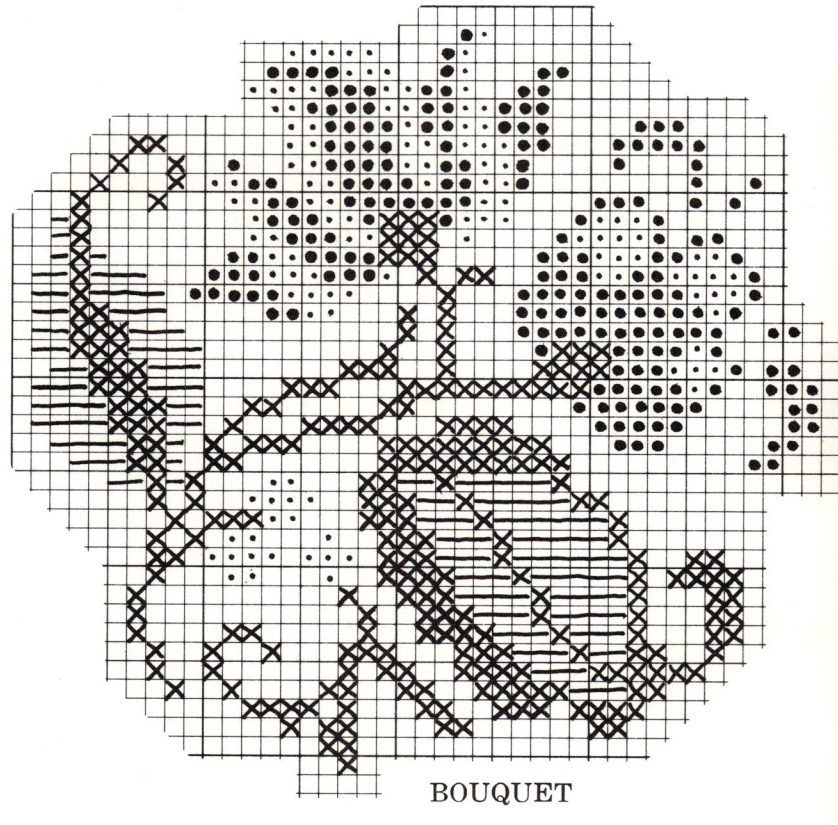

BOUQUET

⊠ green
□ light green
⬤ violet
⊡ lavender

24

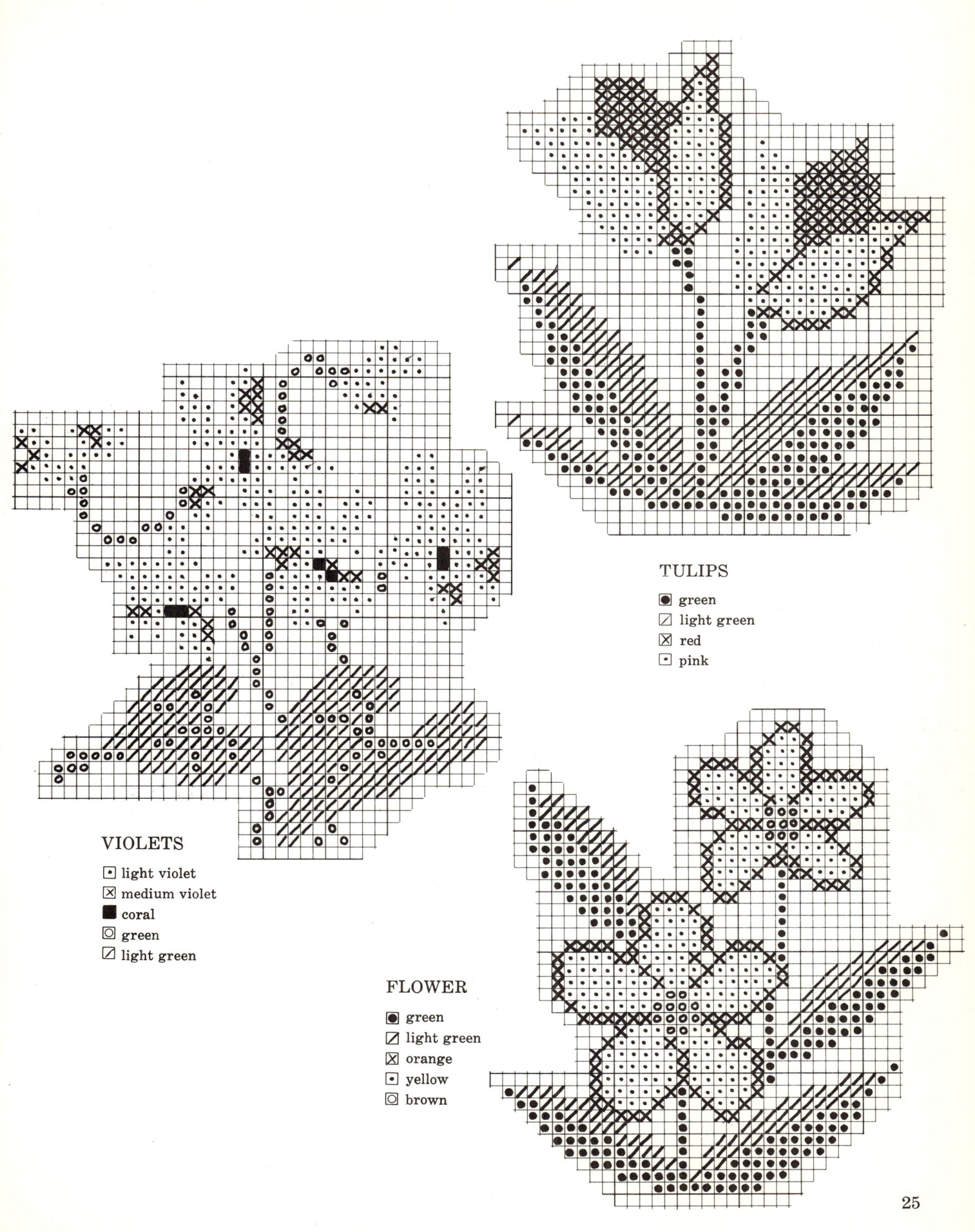

TULIPS

⊙ green
⊘ light green
⊠ red
⊡ pink

VIOLETS

⊡ light violet
⊠ medium violet
■ coral
◉ green
⊘ light green

FLOWER

⊙ green
⊘ light green
⊠ orange
⊡ yellow
◉ brown

25

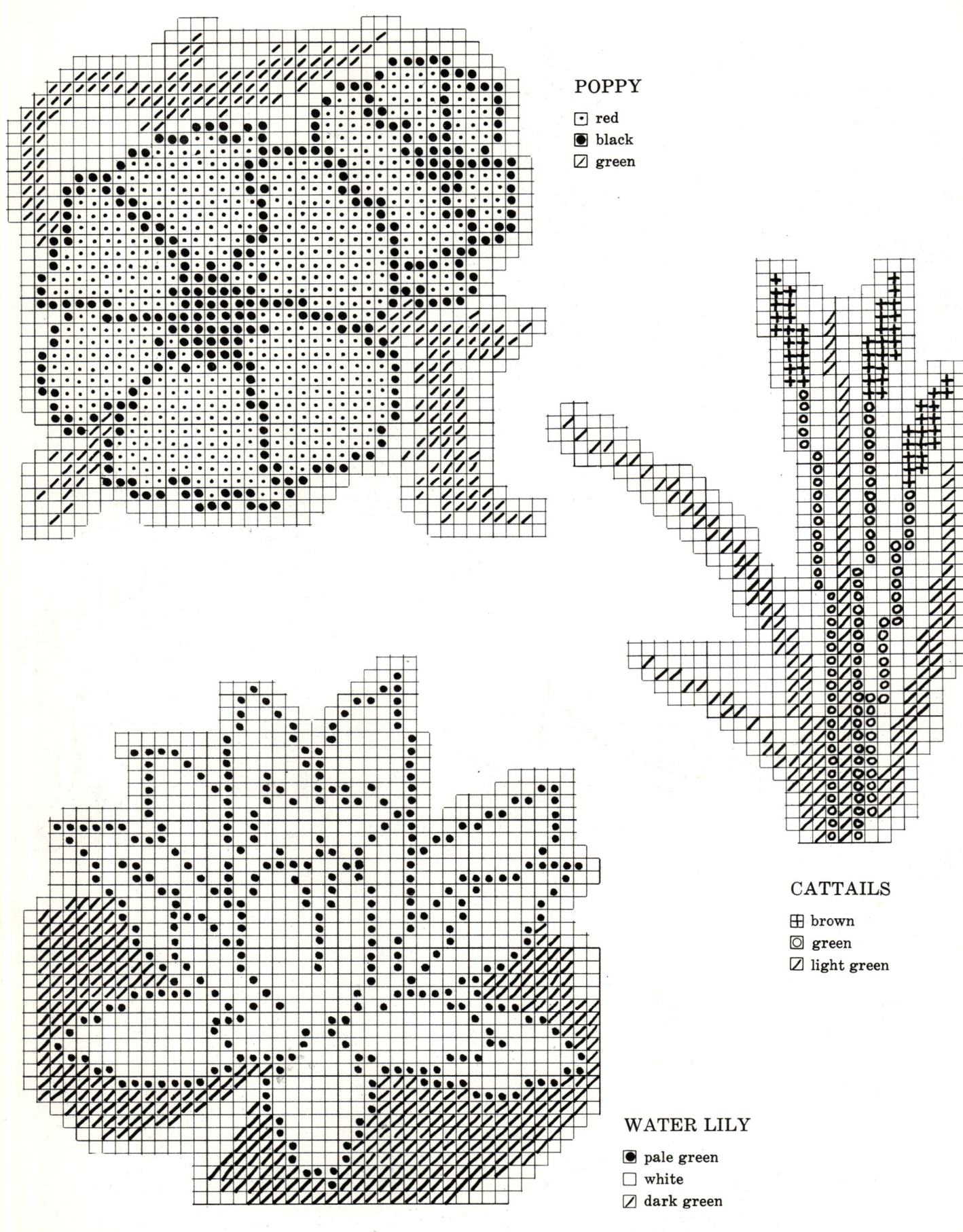

POPPY

⊡ red
◉ black
⧄ green

CATTAILS

⊞ brown
◉ green
⧄ light green

WATER LILY

◉ pale green
☐ white
⧄ dark green

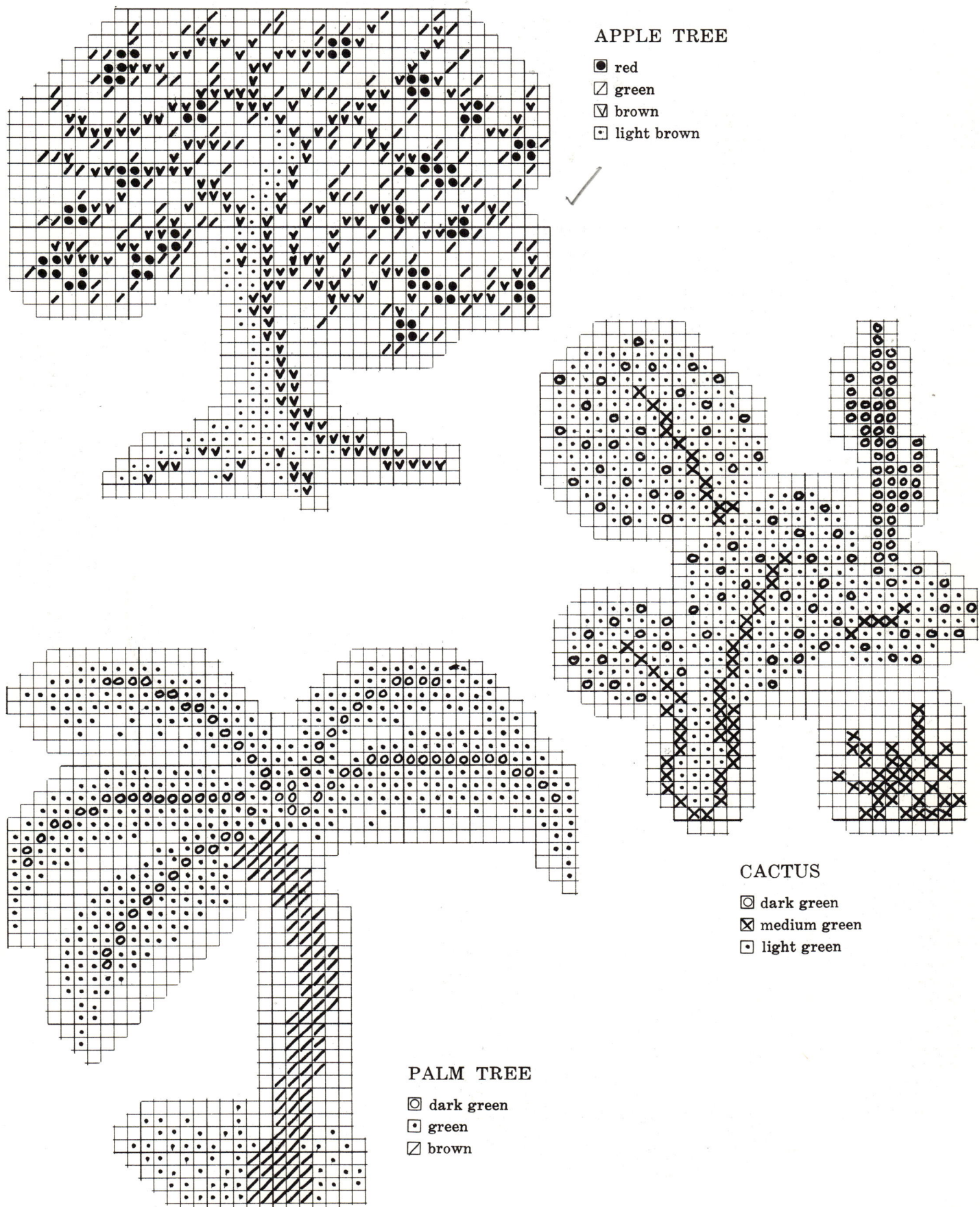

APPLE TREE

- ◉ red
- ⧄ green
- ⬔ brown
- ⊡ light brown

CACTUS

- ◎ dark green
- ⊠ medium green
- ⊡ light green

PALM TREE

- ◎ dark green
- ⊡ green
- ⧄ brown

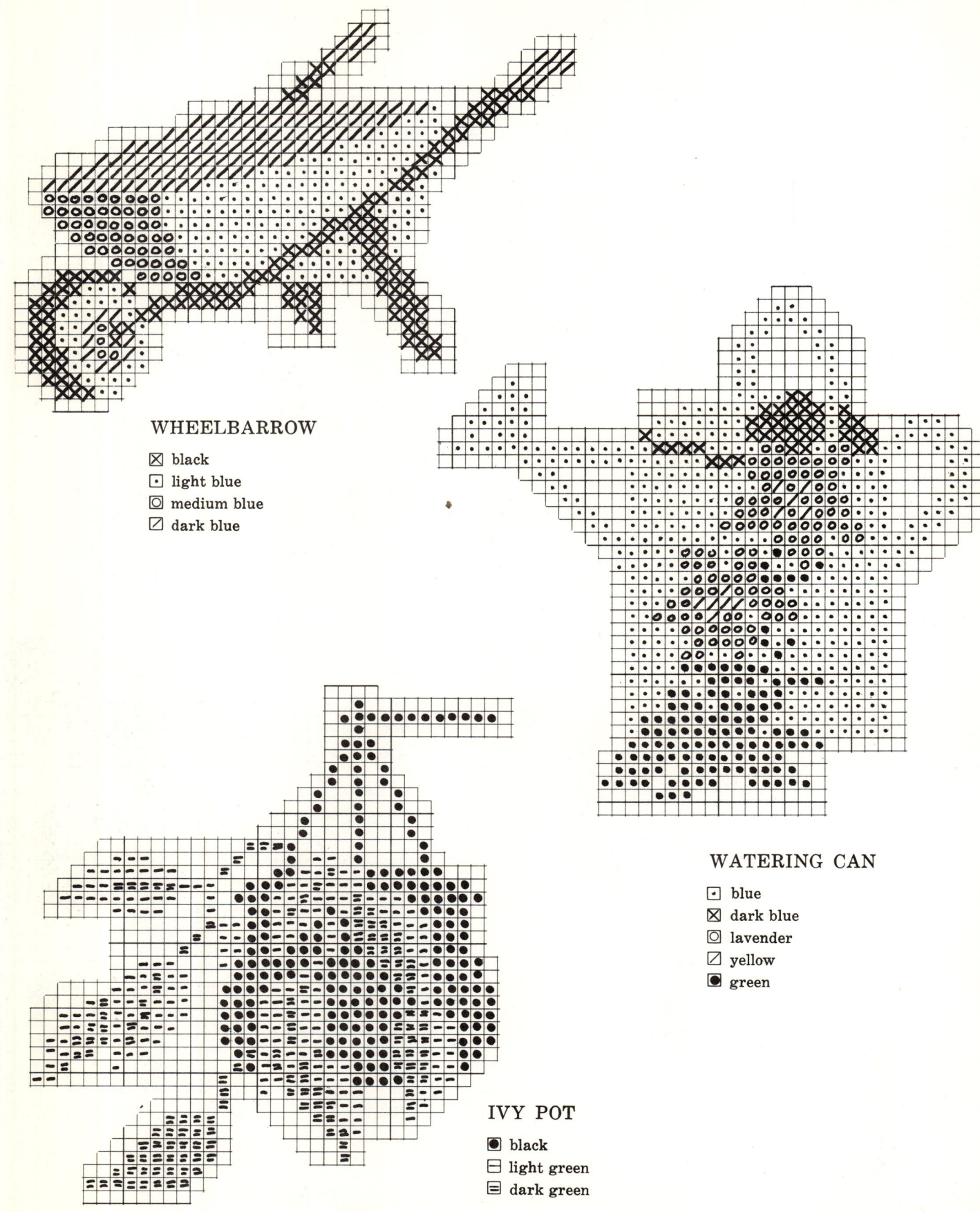

WHEELBARROW

⊠ black
⊡ light blue
⊘ medium blue
⊘ dark blue

WATERING CAN

⊡ blue
⊠ dark blue
⊘ lavender
⊘ yellow
⬤ green

IVY POT

⬤ black
⊟ light green
⊟ dark green

PIANO

☑ black
☐ white

HORN

◎ yellow
◿ dark yellow
● dark gold

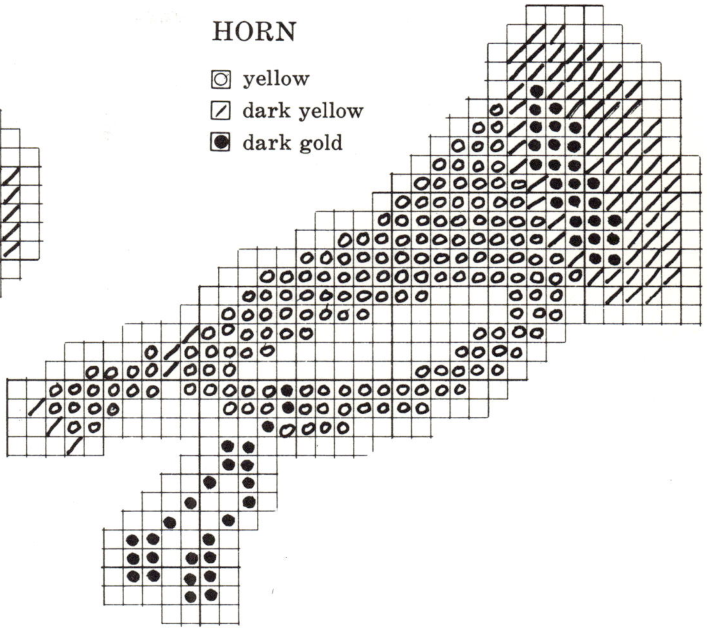

VIOLIN

● dark brown
◿ medium brown
· light brown

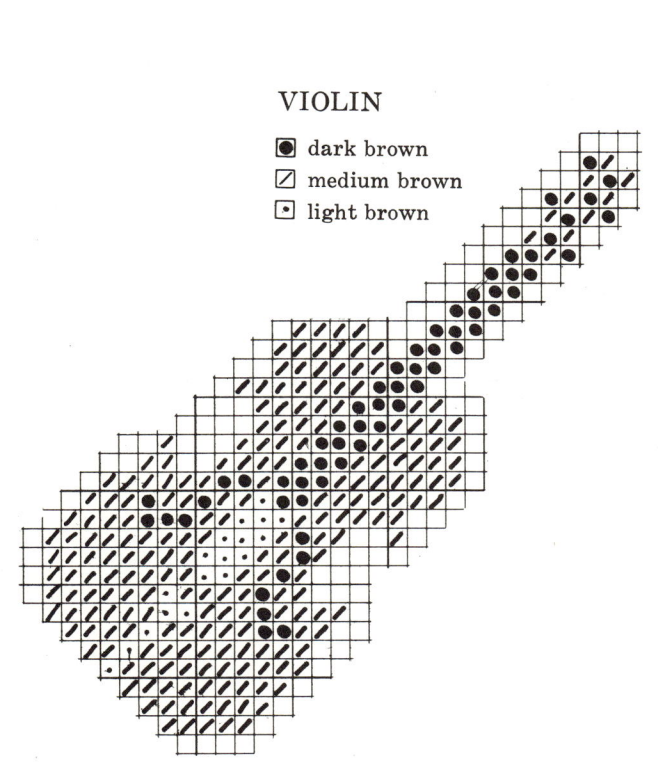

GUITAR

☒ dark brown
· medium brown
◎ light brown

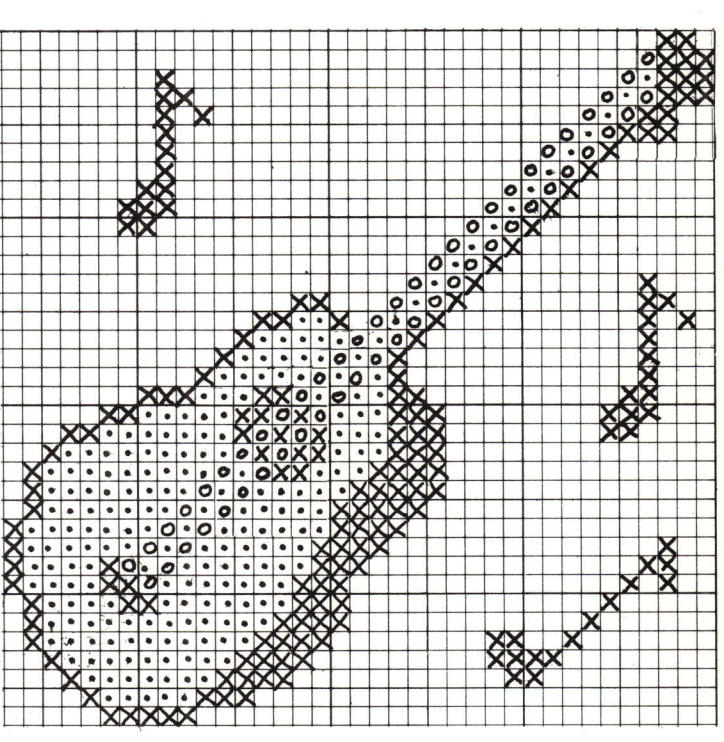

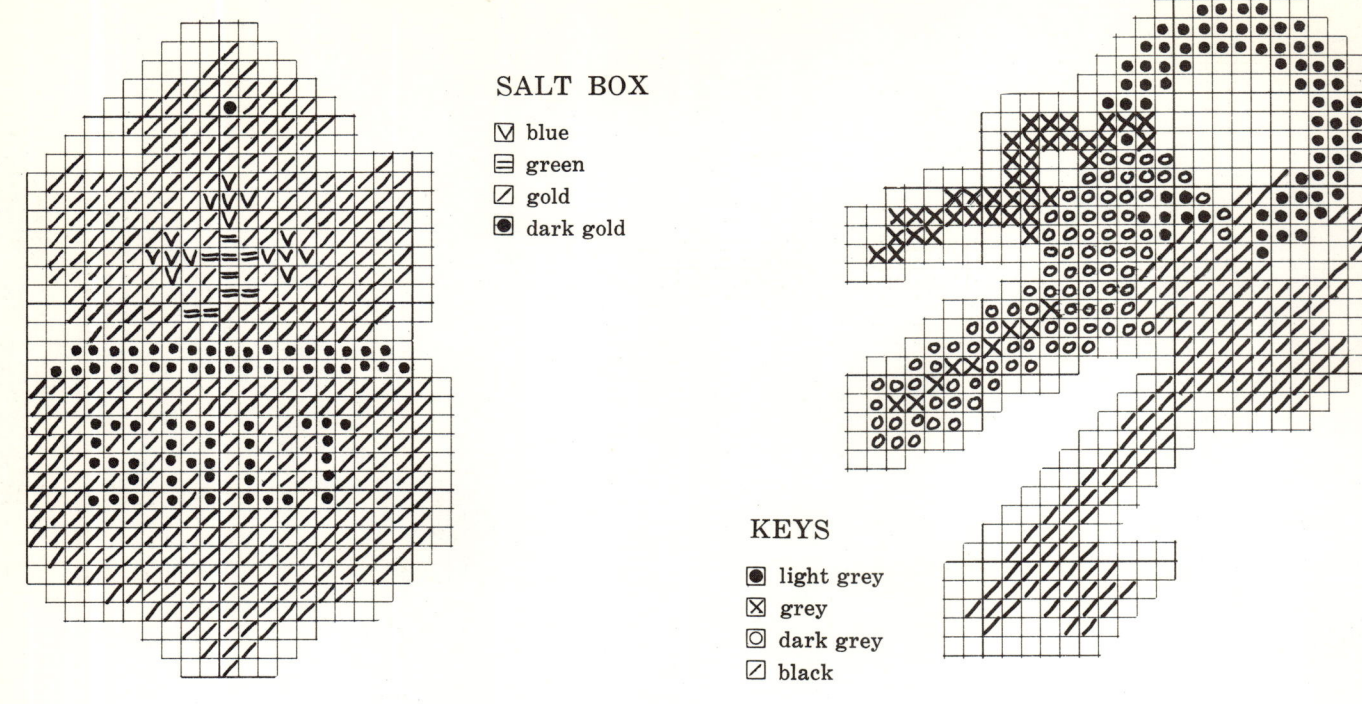

SALT BOX

- ☑ blue
- ☰ green
- ◨ gold
- ◉ dark gold

KEYS

- ◉ light grey
- ☒ grey
- ⊙ dark grey
- ◨ black

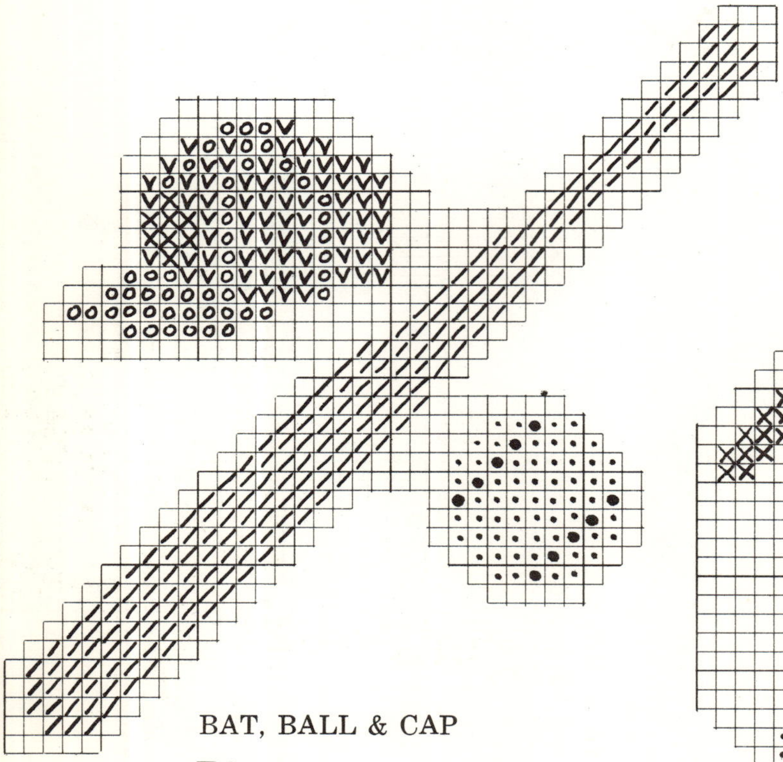

BAT, BALL & CAP

- ◨ brown
- ◉ grey
- · white
- ⊙ red
- ☑ blue
- ☒ yellow

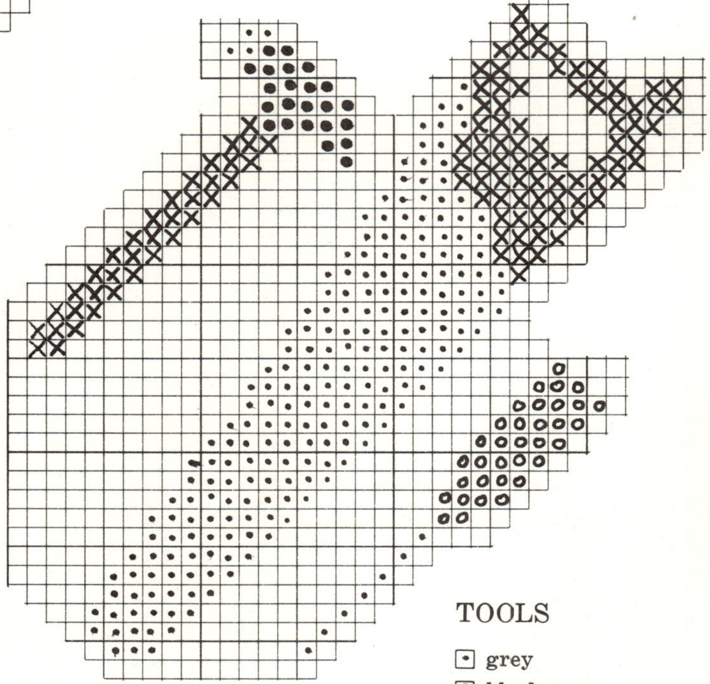

TOOLS

- · grey
- ◉ black
- ☒ brown
- ⊙ orange

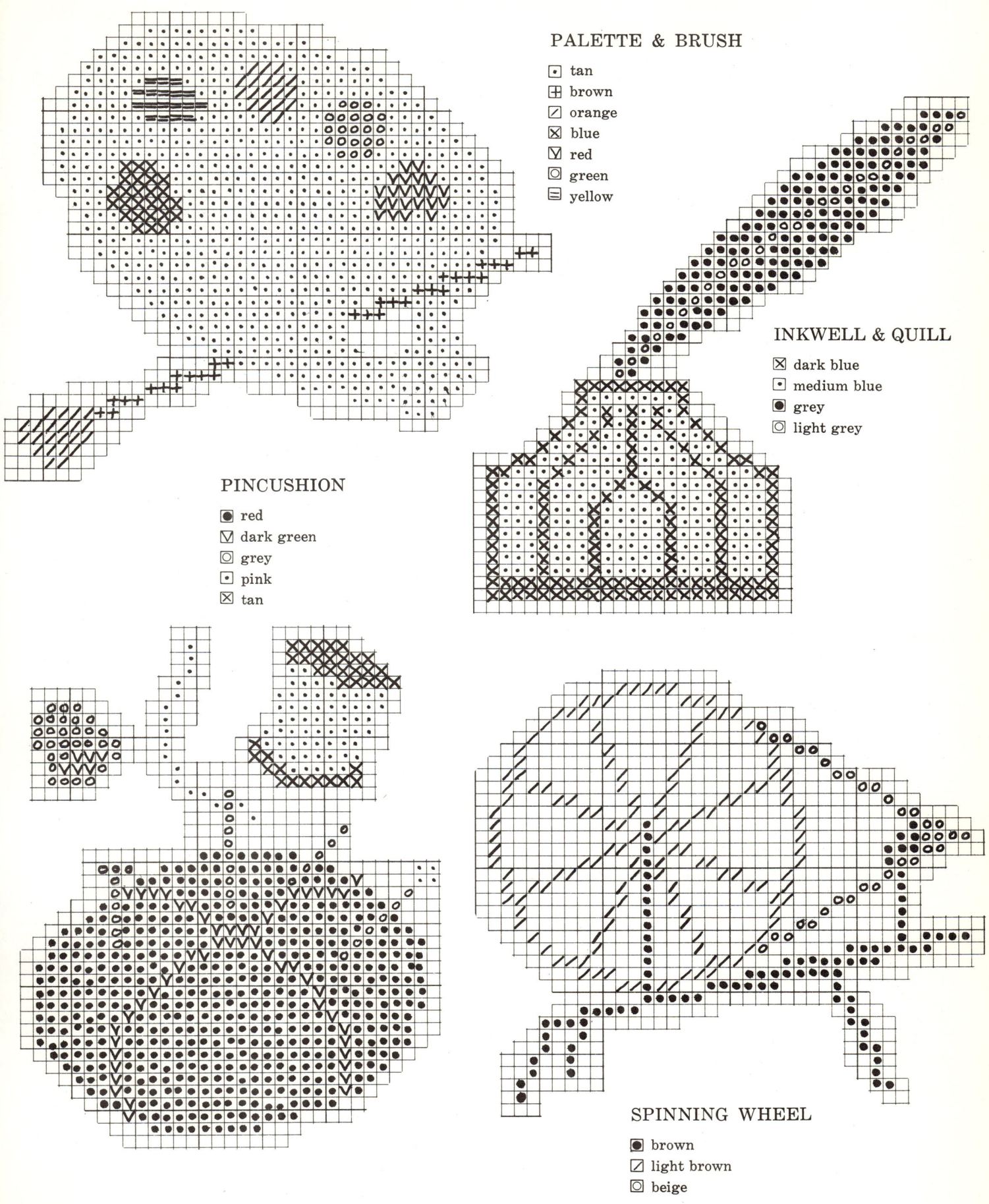

PALETTE & BRUSH

- ⊡ tan
- ⊞ brown
- ⊘ orange
- ⊠ blue
- ⊻ red
- ⊙ green
- ⊟ yellow

INKWELL & QUILL

- ⊠ dark blue
- ⊡ medium blue
- ⬤ grey
- ⊙ light grey

PINCUSHION

- ⬤ red
- ⊻ dark green
- ⊙ grey
- ⊡ pink
- ⊠ tan

SPINNING WHEEL

- ⬤ brown
- ⊘ light brown
- ⊙ beige

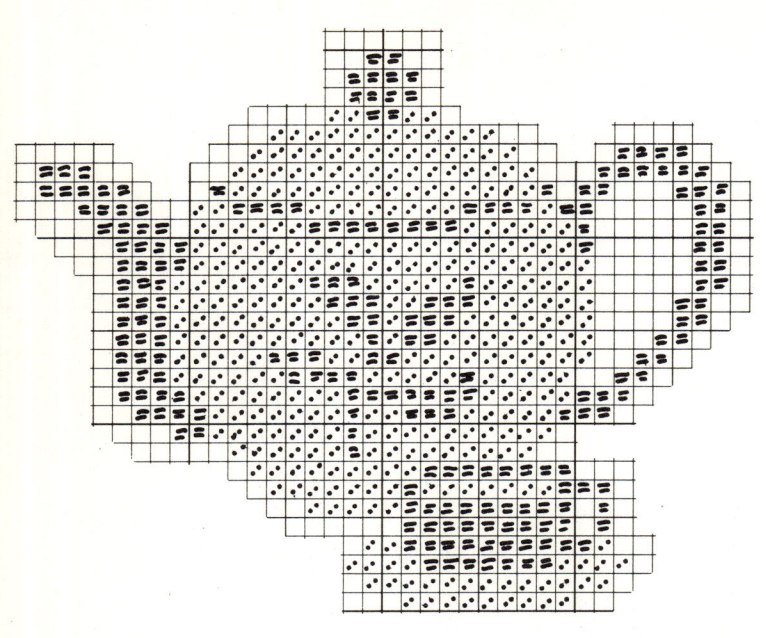

TEAPOT & CUP

⊟ dark green
⊡ yellow

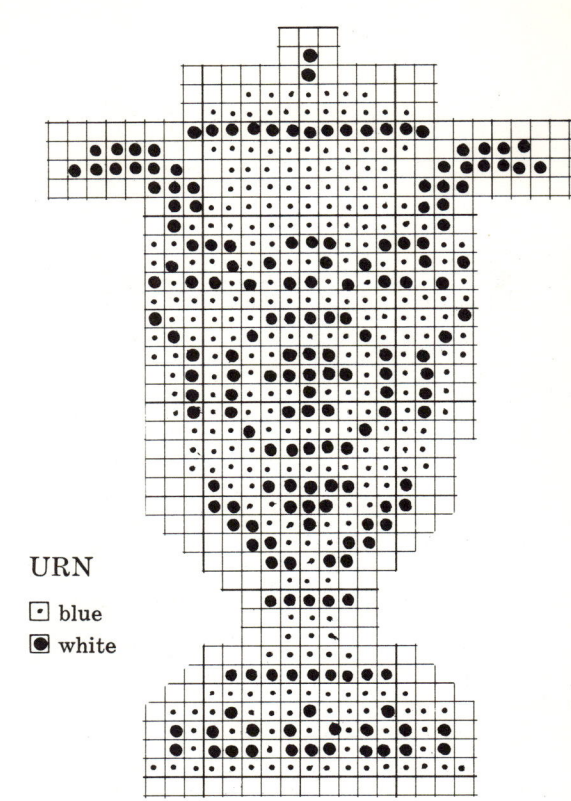

URN

⊡ blue
◉ white

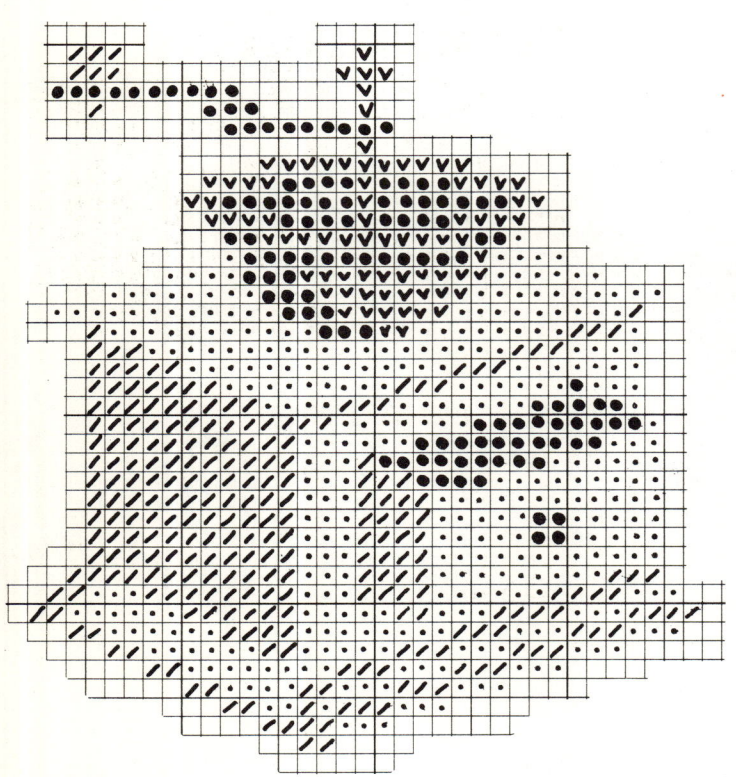

COFFEE GRINDER

◉ black
☑ grey
⊡ light tan
⊘ dark tan

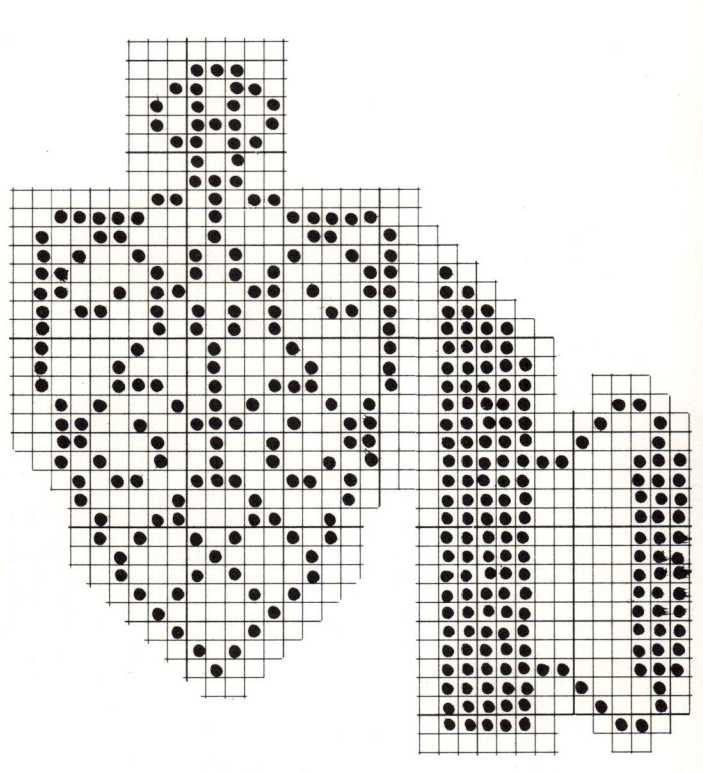

FLATIRON & TRIVET

◉ black

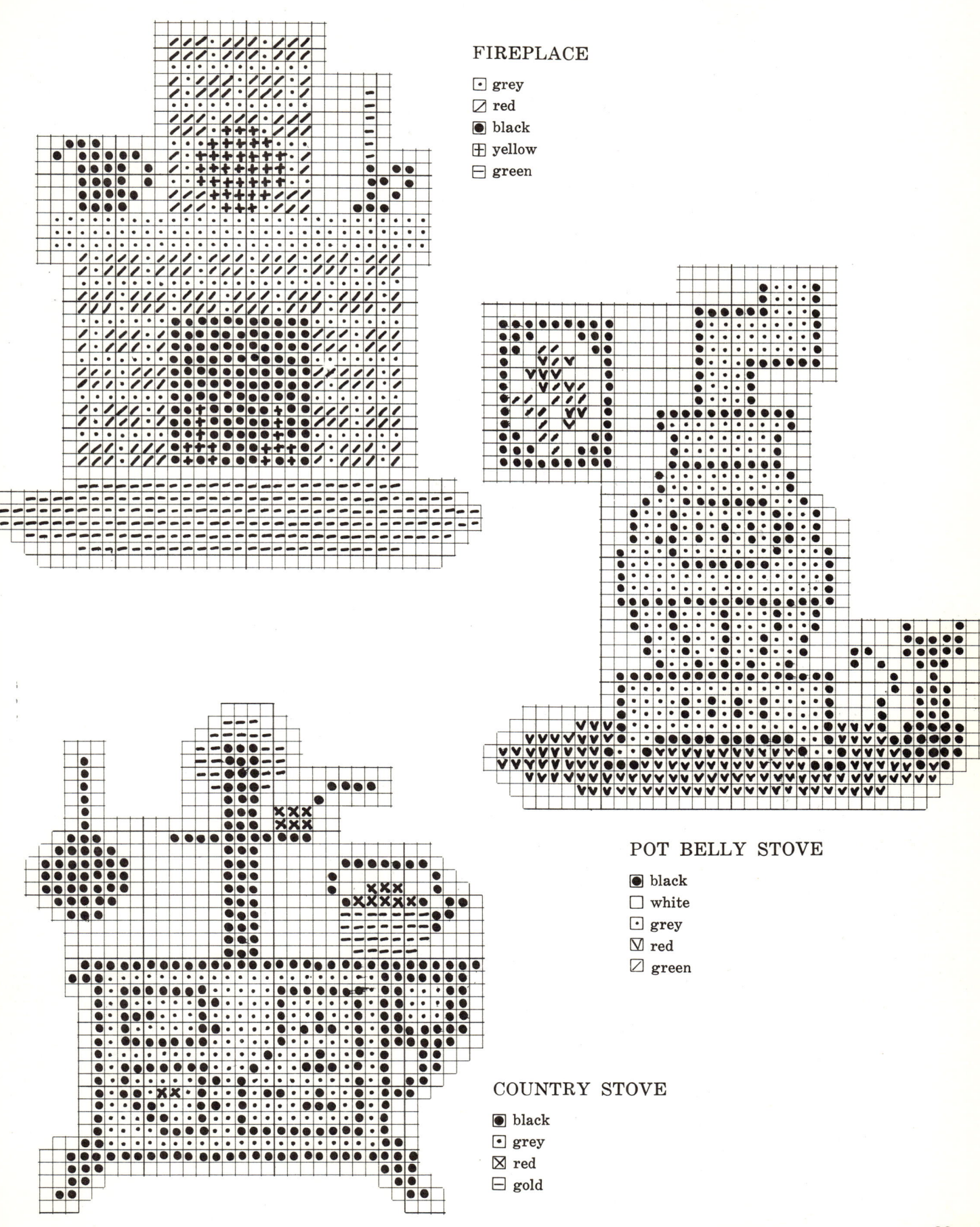

FIREPLACE

- ⊡ grey
- ⧄ red
- ⬤ black
- ⊞ yellow
- ⊟ green

POT BELLY STOVE

- ⬤ black
- ☐ white
- ⊡ grey
- ⧨ red
- ⧄ green

COUNTRY STOVE

- ⬤ black
- ⊡ grey
- ⊠ red
- ⊟ gold

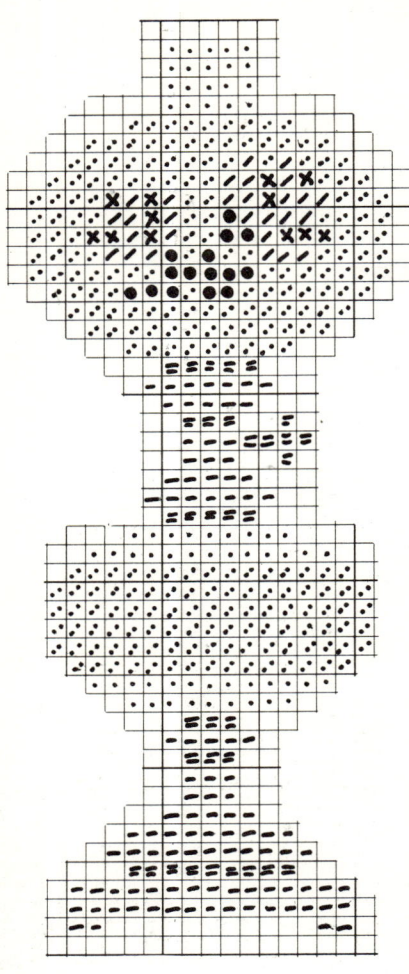

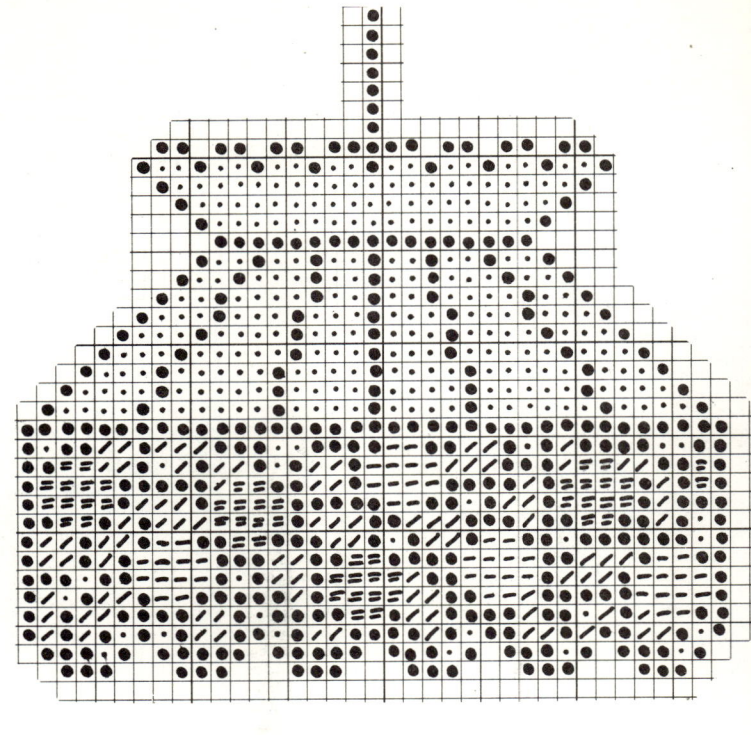

GLOBE LAMP

- ⊡ white
- ⊡ light green
- ⬤ green
- ◿ pink
- ⊠ dark pink
- ⊟ gold
- ⊟ dark gold

TIFFANY LAMP

- ⬤ black
- ⊡ yellow
- ⊟ pink
- ⊟ light pink
- ◿ green

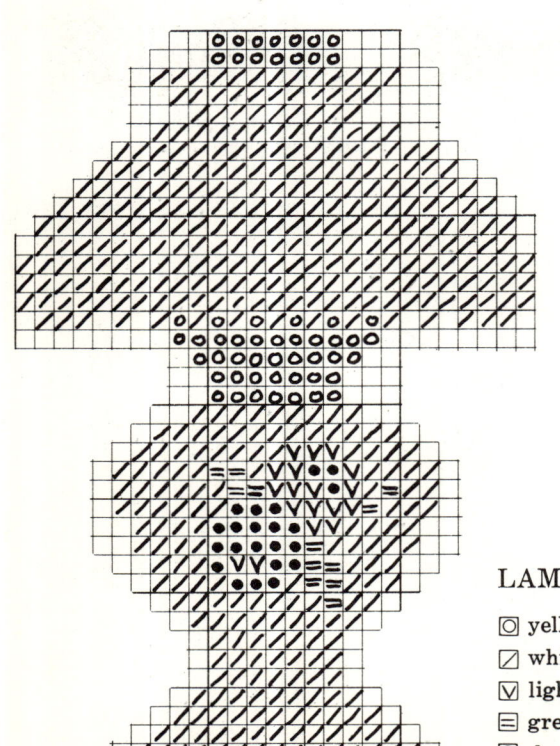

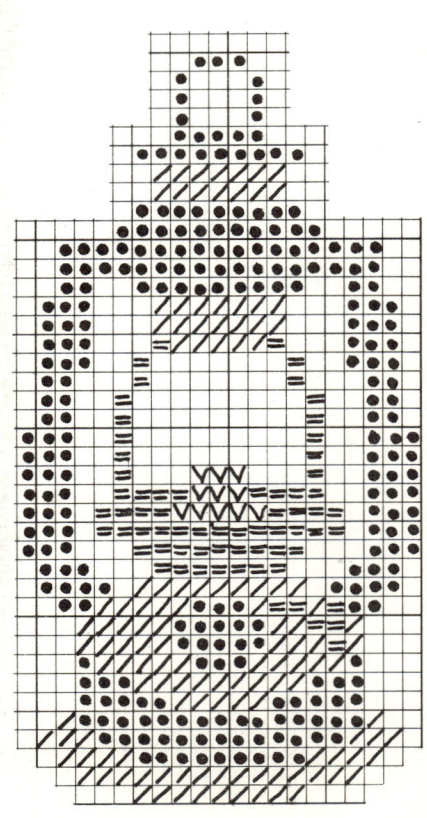

LANTERN

- ⬤ dark green
- ◿ green
- ⊟ black
- ⊻ yellow

LAMP

- ⊚ yellow
- ◿ white
- ⊻ light pink
- ⊟ green
- ⬤ dark pink

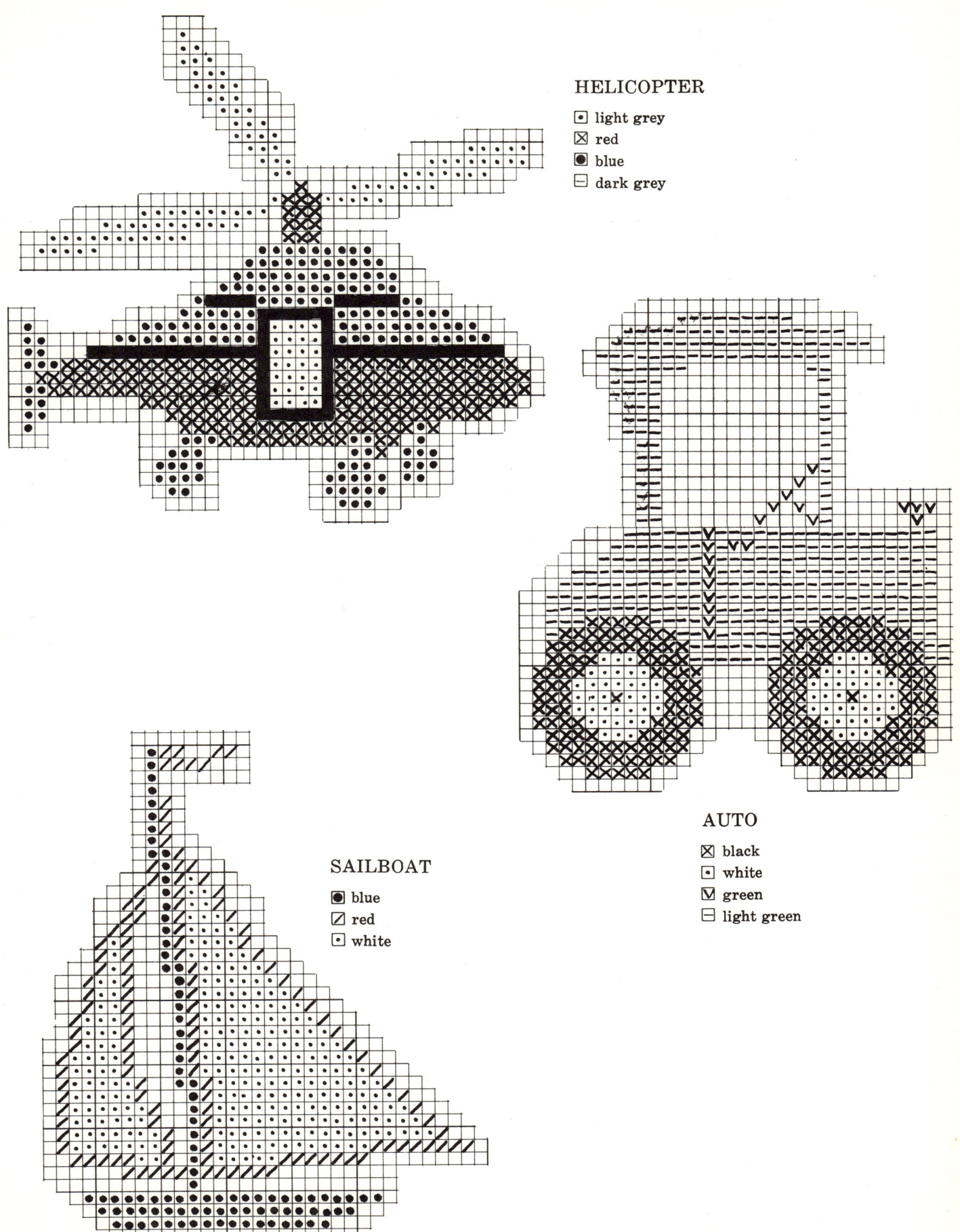

HELICOPTER

- ⊡ light grey
- ⊠ red
- ⬤ blue
- ⊟ dark grey

AUTO

- ⊠ black
- ⊡ white
- Ⅴ green
- ⊟ light green

SAILBOAT

- ⬤ blue
- ⧄ red
- ⊡ white

BIRDBATH GARDEN

Symbol	Color	Symbol	Color
◉	brown	◹	yellow
◿	green	⊠	blue
◎	light brown	⊞	pink
⊡	light green	⊡	light blue

WINDMILL

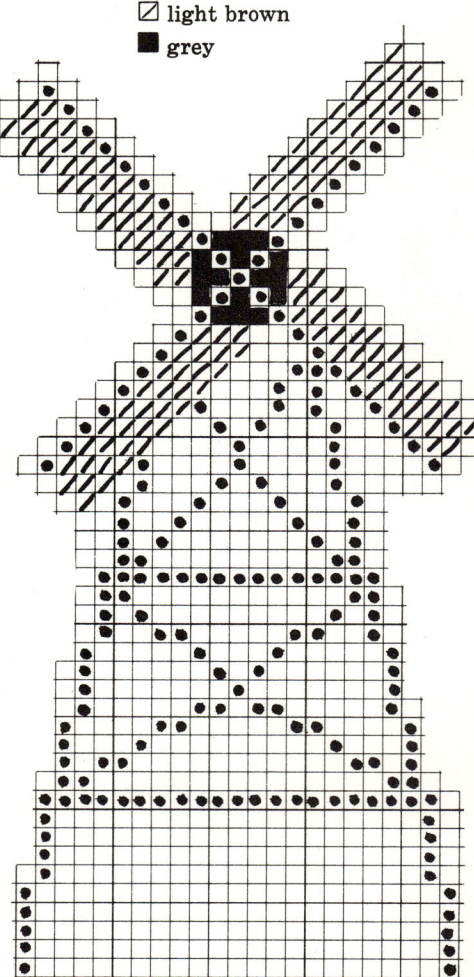

Symbol	Color
◉	dark brown
◿	light brown
■	grey

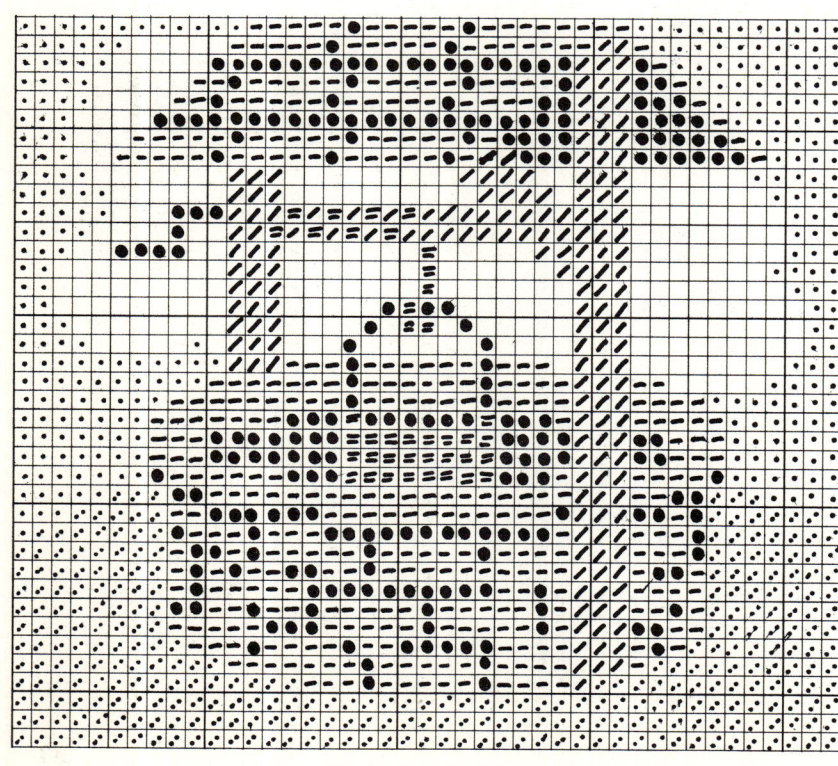

WISHING WELL

Symbol	Color
☐	white
⊟	brown
◿	yellow
◉	black
⊟	red
⊡	blue
⊡	green

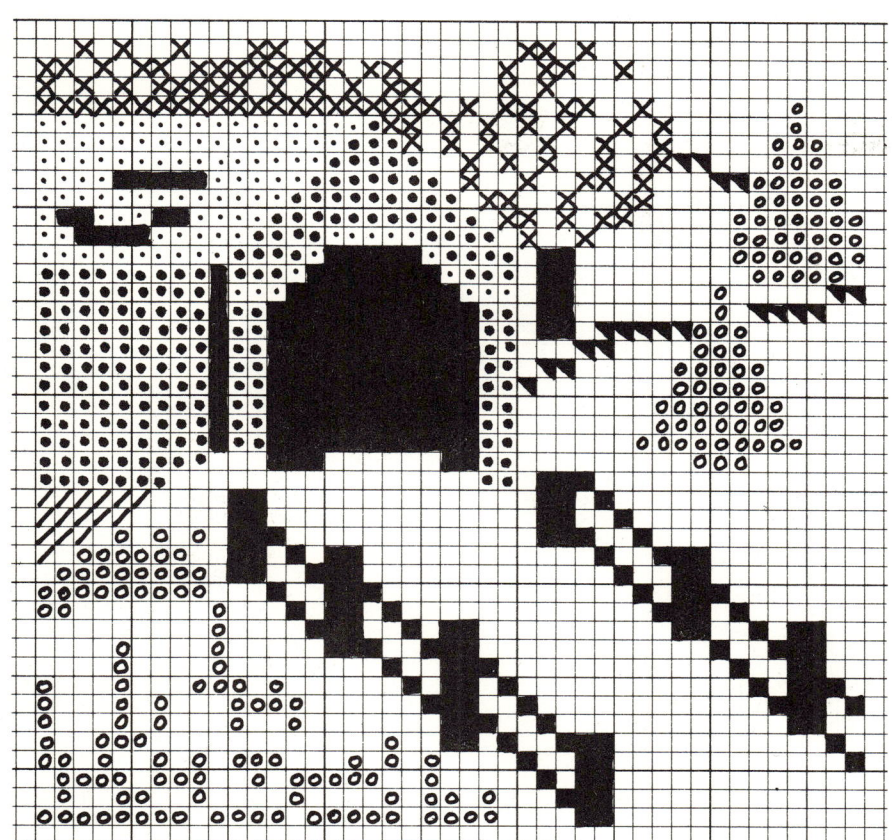

COVERED BRIDGE

Summer		*Winter*	
⊠	medium green	⊠	black
⊙	red	⊘	black
■	black	■	black
⊡	dark green	⊙	red
⊘	light blue	⊡	dark green
⊡	brown	⊡	white
◣	medium green	◣	light grey
☐	light green	☐	white

IN THE COUNTRY

Summer		*Winter*	
◣	medium green	◣	light grey
⊙	dark green	⊙	dark green
⊙	red	⊙	red
⊠	yellow	⊠	yellow
☐	light green	☐	white
■	coral	■	coral
⊞	dark blue	⊞	dark blue
⊟	tan	⊟	tan
⊡	dark blue	⊡	white
⊡	red	⊡	white

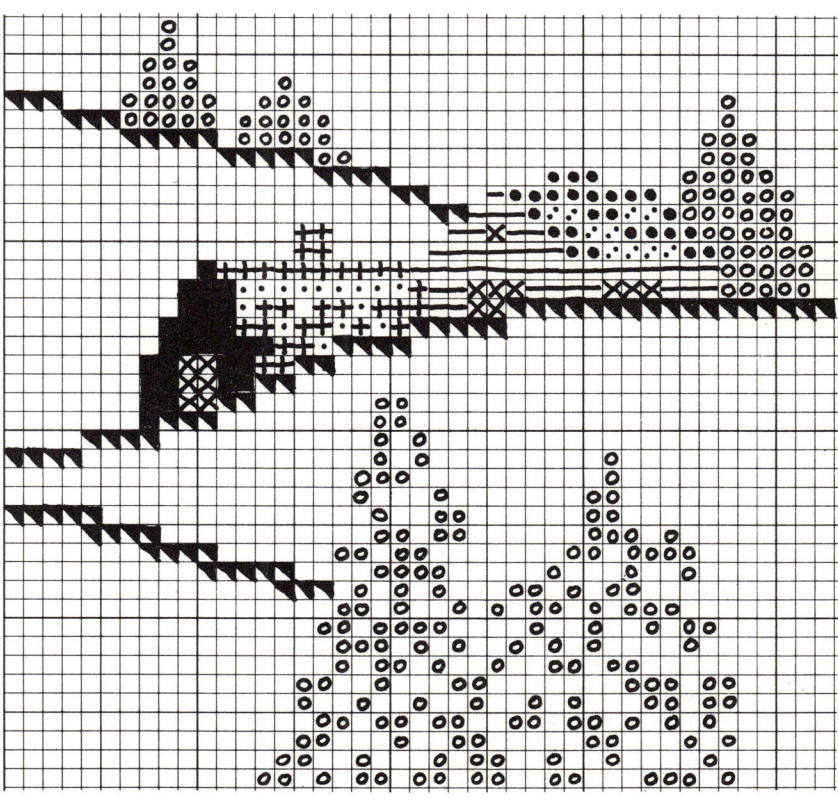

CANDYLAND

Ⓥ light green
⊡ blue
☰ aqua
⊘ pink
⊡ grey
⊟ yellow
● red
☐ white

COUNTRY CHURCH

☐ white
⊘ blue
⊡ yellow
⊠ pink
⊟ grey

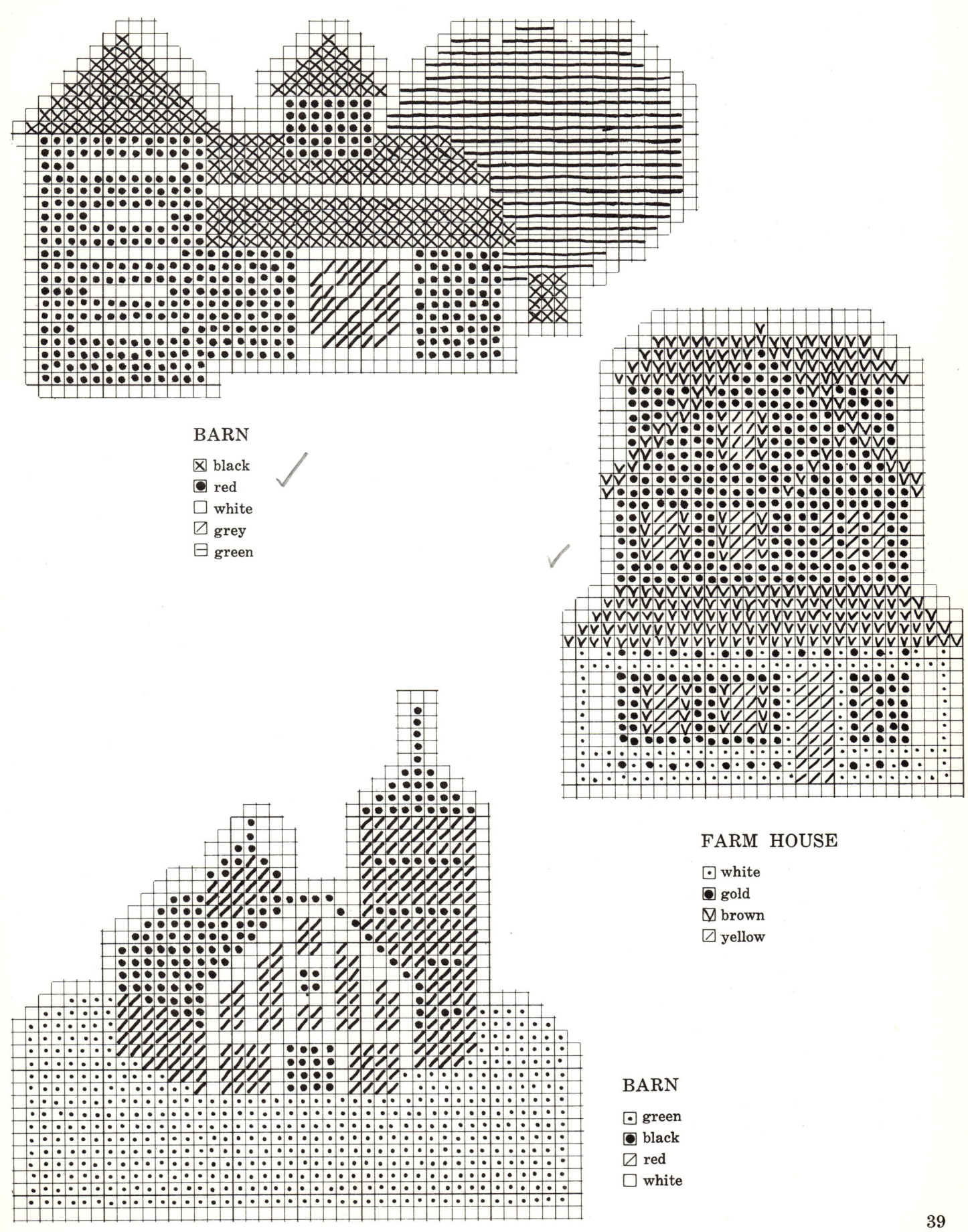

BARN

☒ black ✓
◉ red
☐ white
◩ grey
⊟ green

FARM HOUSE

⊡ white
◉ gold
Ⅴ brown
◪ yellow

BARN

⊡ green
◉ black
◪ red
☐ white

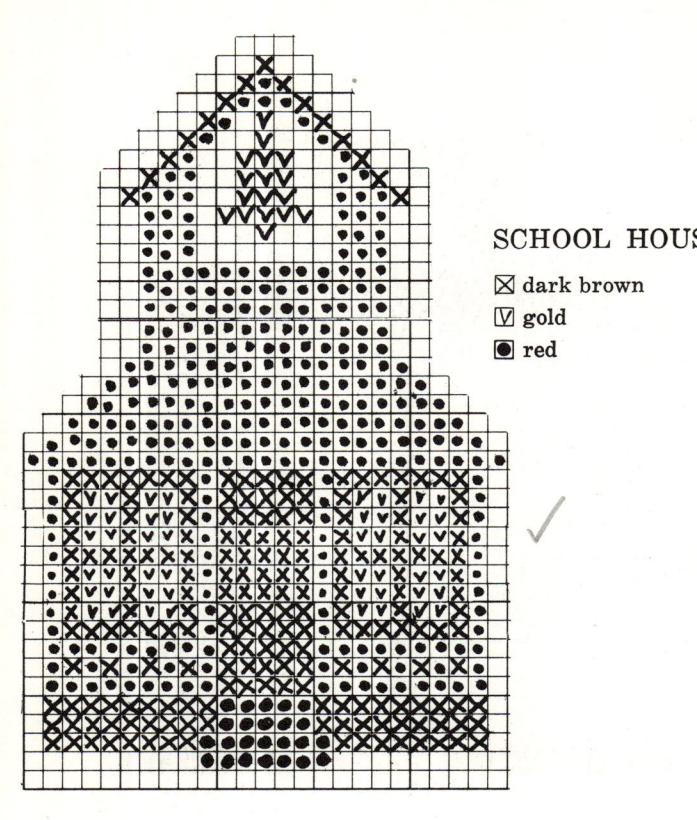

SCHOOL HOUSE

- ⊠ dark brown
- Ⅴ gold
- ⦿ red

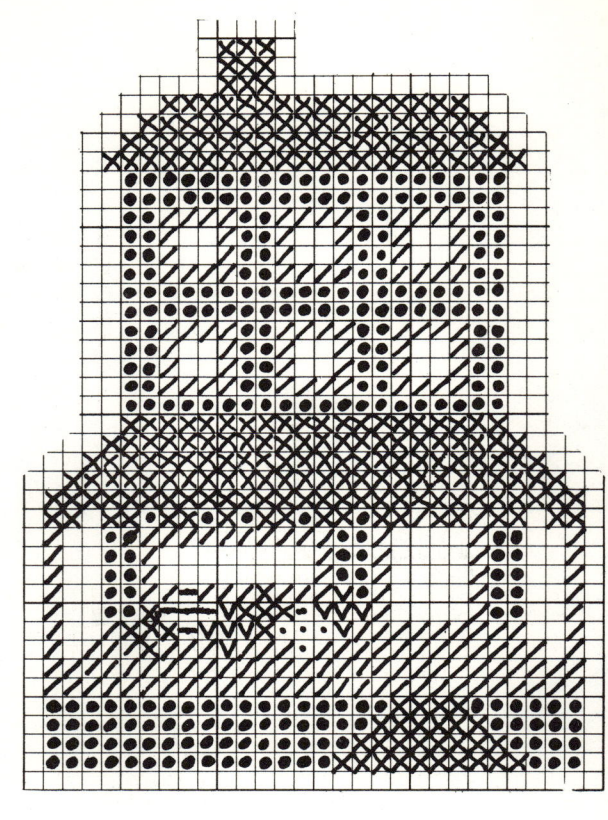

COUNTRY STORE

- ⊠ red
- ⦿ tan
- ⧄ brown
- ⊟ green
- ⊡ yellow
- Ⅴ orange

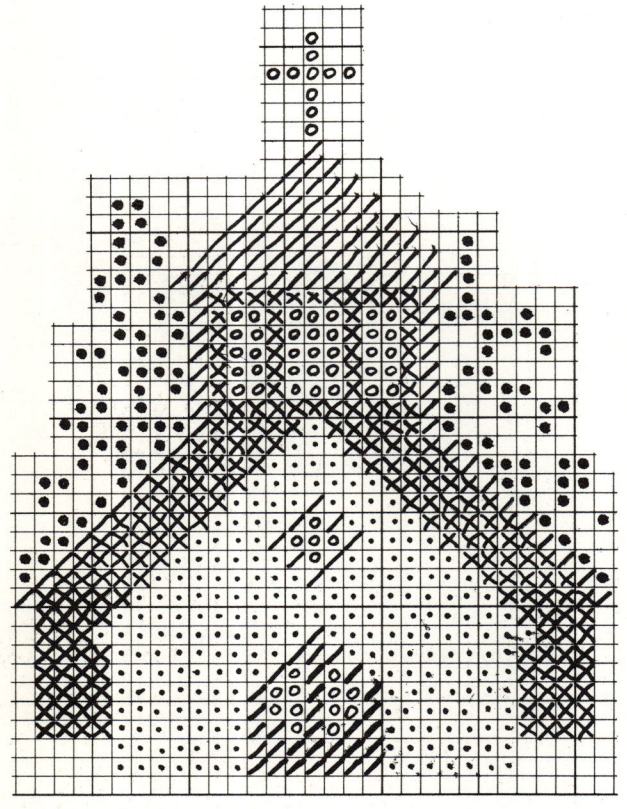

VICTORIAN HOUSE

- ⊡ white
- ◎ medium blue
- ⦿ light blue
- ⧄ yellow
- ■ dark blue

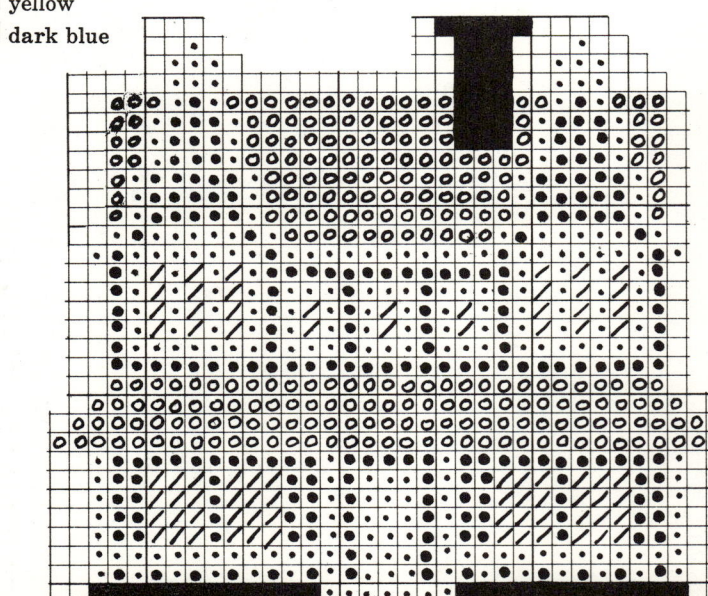

COUNTRY CHURCH

- ⊡ tan
- ⦿ green
- ⊠ medium brown
- ⧄ dark brown
- ◎ yellow

VICTORIAN HOUSE

- ⊡ white
- ⊚ beige
- ◉ light brown
- ⊘ yellow
- Ⅴ medium brown
- ■ dark brown

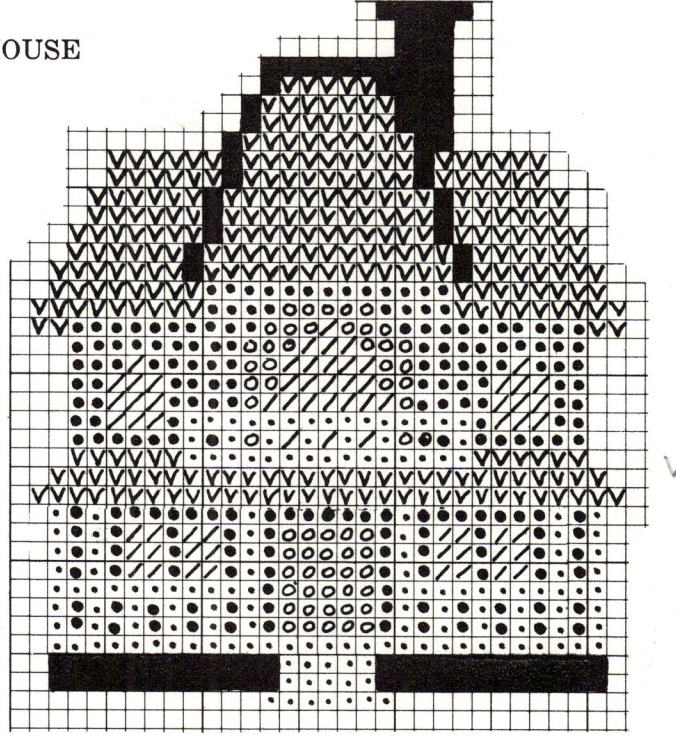

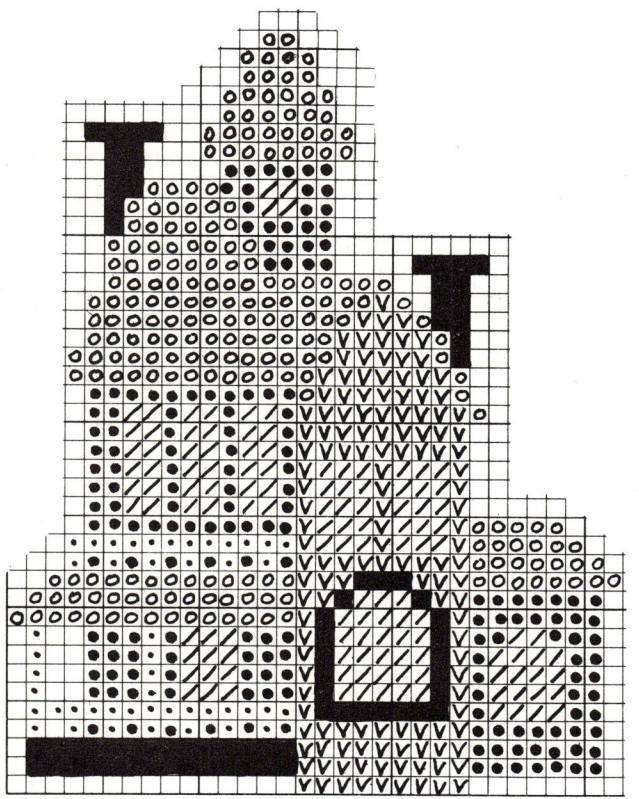

VICTORIAN HOUSE

- ⊡ white
- ⊚ green
- ◉ gold
- ⊘ yellow
- Ⅴ dark gold
- ■ dark green

VICTORIAN HOUSE

- ⊡ white
- ◉ grey
- ⊘ yellow
- Ⅴ dark grey

41

MORE CHARTED DESIGN BOOKS FROM DOVER

CHARTED DESIGNS FOR NEEDLE-MADE RUGS, Sibyl I. Mathews. 45 charted designs ready to transfer onto rug canvas: dolphins, tulips, toy soldiers, Manx motifs, many more. Full instructions; 44 additional illustrations. 150pp. 7⅞ x 10¾. 23264-6 Pa. **$4.00**

CHARTED PEASANT DESIGNS FROM SAXON TRANSYLVANIA, Heinz E. Kiewe. 195 authentic cross-stitch designs, 11th through early 20th century. Birds, flowers, geometric patterns, mythical beasts, more. Detailed introduction identifies symbols, patterns. 64pp. 8¼ x 11. 23425-8 Pa. **$2.00**

A TREASURY OF CHARTED DESIGNS FOR NEEDLEWORKERS, Georgia L. Gorham and Jeanne M. Warth. 141 motifs charted for ready use include lovebirds, cat with yarn, toy train, pansies, windmill, etc. Designs most prized by needleworkers. Instructions. Color key. 48pp. 8¼ x 11. 23558-0 Pa. **$1.75**

CHARTED MONOGRAMS FOR NEEDLEPOINT AND CROSS-STITCH, Rita Weiss. 350 striking turn-of-the-century monograms, taken from a rare Viennese album. Also includes many crowns, complete sets of Roman and Arabic numerals. 48pp. 8¼ x 11. 23555-6 Pa. **$1.50**

CHARTED SWISS FOLK DESIGNS, Elvira Parolini-Ruffini. Lovely charted versions of crowns, stars, flowers, hunting scenes, etc., collected from the Engadine Valley in the Swiss canton of Grisons. Magnificent folk art. 32pp. 8¼ x 11. (Available in U.S. only) 23574-2 Pa. **$1.50**

CLASSIC POSTERS FOR NEEDLEPOINT, Elizabeth Irvine. 22 classic art posters by Mucha, Will Bradley, the Beggarstaffs, charted for any variety of needlepoint. Yarn and canvas requirements, authentic color schemes provided. 48pp. 8¼ x 11. 23640-4 Pa. **$1.75**

NEEDLEPOINT DESIGNS AFTER ILLUSTRATIONS BY BEATRIX POTTER, Rita Weiss. 24 popular Beatrix Potter scenes, characters charted for needlepoint or counted thread embroidery. All reproduced in full-color needlepoint on covers. 32pp. 8¼ x 11. (Available in U.S. only) 20218-6 Pa. **$1.50**

CHRISTMAS NEEDLEPOINT DESIGNS, Rita Weiss. 36 original seasonal designs including 12 Days of Christmas series. Graphed for ready transfer onto # 10 needlepoint canvas. Instructions for gift projects. 36 cover illustrations. 32pp. 8¼ x 11. 23161-5 Pa. **$1.50**

BAROQUE CHARTED DESIGNS FOR NEEDLEWORK, Johan Sibmacher. 36 plates reprinted from 1604 Nuremberg needlework patterns. All graphed. Geometrics, heraldic, mythological and religious designs. 99 motifs total. 48pp. 8¼ x 11. 23186-0 Pa. **$1.75**

PERSIAN RUG MOTIFS FOR NEEDLEPOINT CHARTED FOR EASY USE, Lyatif Kerimov. 160 motifs from Russian-Iranian borderlands. Birds, florals, animals, border designs, more, in traditional renderings. 45 plates. 48pp. 8¼ x 11. 23187-9 Pa. **$2.00**

AFRICAN NEEDLEPOINT DESIGNS CHARTED FOR EASY USE, Diana Oliver Turner. 45 designs based on the rich African art tradition: masks, animals, birds, geometrics, etc. Charted for easy use in needlepoint or counted thread embroidery. 25 color illustrations altogether. 41pp. 8¼ x 11. 23244-1 Pa. **$2.00**

PENNSYLVANIA DUTCH NEEDLEPOINT DESIGNS CHARTED FOR EASY USE, Marcia Loeb. 50 authentic designs suitable for pillows, belts, pictures, etc. All charted for easy use in needlepoint and counted thread embroidery. 22 designs rendered in full-color needlepoint on covers. 48pp. 8¼ x 11. 23299-9 Pa. **$1.75**

NEEDLEWORK ALPHABETS AND DESIGNS, edited by Blanche Cirker. 27 alphabets, many geometric designs, animals, butterflies, pictorial materials printed in 2 colors on grids for easy use. Dillmont material, very beautiful. 85pp. (Available in U.S. only) 23159-3 Pa. **$2.25**

GEOMETRIC NEEDLEPOINT DESIGNS, Carol Belanger Grafton. 43 imaginative charted designs, all original, produce striking color effects, op art, even visual illusions. 16 color designs on covers. Instructions. 41pp. 8¼ x 11. 23160-7 Pa. **$1.75**

FAVORITE ILLUSTRATIONS FROM CHILDREN'S CLASSICS IN COUNTED CROSS-STITCH, Ginnie Thompson. Famous needlewoman offers 28 sewing pictures from Tenniel's *Alice*, Denslow's *Wizard of Oz*, Kate Greenaway. 42pp. 8¼ x 11. 23394-4 Pa. **$1.50**

PATCHWORK QUILT DESIGNS FOR NEEDLEPOINT CHARTED FOR EASY USE, Frank Fontana. 41 traditional quilt block patterns selected and adapted; capture early American flavor, striking modern effects. Full general directions. Historical captions. Each charted on 7½ x 7½-inch square. Repeat or combine for almost any size project. 48pp. 8¼ x 11. 23300-6 Pa. **$1.50**

FULL-COLOR AMERICAN INDIAN DESIGNS FOR NEEDLEPOINT RUGS CHARTED FOR EASY USE, Dorothy Story. 32 plates of authentic material, all in full color; charted for # 5 canvas, but also other applications. Pillows, rugs, hangings, etc. 32pp. 8¼ x 11. 23190-9 Pa. **$2.00**

FULL-COLOR FLORAL NEEDLEPOINT DESIGNS CHARTED FOR EASY USE, Eva Costabel-Deutsch. Startling oversized blooms, delicate sprays, intriguing bouquetlike combinations, and Art Deco elaborations of floral motifs: 32 designs in full, vibrant colors, charted for easy use on # 10 needlepoint canvas. 32pp. 8¼ x 11. 23387-1 Pa. **$2.50**

AMERICAN INDIAN NEEDLEPOINT DESIGNS FOR PILLOWS, BELTS, HANDBAGS AND OTHER PROJECTS, Roslyn Epstein. 37 authentic American Indian designs adapted for modern needlepoint projects. Grid backing makes designs easily transferable to canvas. 48pp. 8¼ x 11. 22973-4 Pa. **$1.50**

VICTORIAN NEEDLEPOINT DESIGNS FROM GODEY'S LADY'S BOOK AND PETERSON'S MAGAZINE, Godey's Lady's Book. Edited by Rita Weiss. Unique, remarkable pictorial needlepoint, on grids, from finest sources: 43 in all, bicyclists, cats, horses, sea scenes, dancers, overall designs, etc. Instructions. 36pp. 8¼ x 11. 23163-1 Pa. **$1.75**

FULL-COLOR BICENTENNIAL NEEDLEPOINT DESIGNS, Carol Belanger Grafton. 32 full-color charted designs: slogans and flags, portrait of Washington, minuteman and drummer boy, cannon, Paul Revere's ride, other patriotic designs inspired by the Bicentennial. Full instructions. 32pp. in full color. 8¼ x 11. 23233-6 Pa. **$2.00**

FULL-COLOR RUSSIAN FOLK NEEDLEPOINT DESIGNS CHARTED FOR EASY USE, Frieda Halpern. 31 full-page, full-color designs are adapted from Russian folk designs. Elegant yet child-like riders on horseback, mythical beasts, birds, florals, geometric patterns. Charted for easy use on # 10 needlepoint canvas. Instructions. 32pp. 8¼ x 11. 23451-7 Pa. **$2.95**

CHARTED FOLK DESIGNS FOR CROSS-STITCH EMBROIDERY, Maria Foris & Andreas Foris. 278 charted folk designs, most in 2 colors, from Danube region: florals, fantastic beasts, geometrics, traditional symbols, more. Border and central patterns. 77pp. 8¼ x 11. 23191-7 Pa. **$2.95**

ANNE ORR'S CHARTED DESIGNS, Anne Orr. Over 100 best designs by premier needlework designer, all on charts: flowers, borders, birds, children, alphabets, etc. Widely bought 1910 to 1945, still sought after today. Over 100 charts, 10 in color, and 7 photos. Total of 40pp. 8¼ x 11. 23704-4 Pa. **$1.75**

Paperbound unless otherwise indicated. Prices subject to change without notice. Available at your book dealer or write for free catalogues to Dept. Needlework 15, Dover Publications Inc., 180 Varick St., N.Y., N.Y. 10014. Please indicate your field of interest. Each year Dover publishes over 150 books on music, fine art, science, languages, chess, puzzles, nature, anthropology, antiques, folklore, art instruction, crafts, needlework, and other areas.

Manufactured in the U.S.A.